D0628997

The Way of the World

THE NEW MERMAIDS

General Editor

BRIAN GIBBONS
Professor of English Literature, University of Zürich

Previous general editors of the series have been
PHILIP BROCKBANK
BRIAN MORRIS
ROMA GILL

G. Kneller Bar.t pinx.t

T. Chambars sculp.

The Way of the World

WILLIAM CONGREVE

Edited by
BRIAN GIBBONS
Professor of English Literature
University of Zürich

LONDON/A & C BLACK

NEW YORK/W W NORTON

Reprinted 1986, 1988
by A & C Black (Publishers) Limited
35 Bedford Row, London WC1R 4JH

First published in this form 1971
by Ernest Benn Limited

© *Ernest Benn Limited 1971*

Published in the United States of America by
W. W. Norton and Company Inc.
500 Fifth Avenue, New York, N. Y. 10110

Printed in Great Britain by
Whitstable Litho Ltd., Whitstable, Kent

British Library Cataloguing in Publication Data

Congreve, William, *b.1670*
The way of the world.—(The New Mermaids).
1. Title 2. Gibbons, Brian, *date*
3. Series
822′.4 PR3364.W3

ISBN 0-7136-2898-7
ISBN 0-393-90004-5 (U.S.A.)

CONTENTS

Acknowledgements	ix
Introduction	xi
The Author	xi
The Play	xvii
The Sources	xxxi
The Text	xxxiii
Further Reading	xxxv
THE WAY OF THE WORLD	1
Dedication	3
Prologue	7
Dramatis Personae	9
Text	11
Epilogue	115

ACKNOWLEDGEMENTS

AMONG MODERN editions of *The Way of the World* I have most frequently consulted those by Montague Summers, Kathleen Lynch, and Herbert Davis; I have referred to them occasionally in the commentary to the present edition by their editors' surnames. I owe much to the biographical study of Congreve by John C. Hodges (*William Congreve: Letters and Documents*) and something also to discussions at the symposium on Congreve held in September 1970 at the University of York.

The present edition has been prepared with the help of photocopies and books, for the use of which I have to thank the Directors of the British Museum and the Librarians of the University of Cambridge and the University of York. In conclusion I would like to thank the General Editors for their assistance.

York BRIAN GIBBONS
June 1971

INTRODUCTION

THE AUTHOR

WILLIAM CONGREVE was born in Yorkshire on 24 January 1670,[1] but spent his youth in Ireland, where his father served as a lieutenant in the English garrisons at Youghal and Carrickfergus, being transferred when Congreve was twelve to Kilkenny, where the boy was able to attend one of the best schools in the British Isles. From there in April 1686 Congreve went as a classical scholar to Trinity College, Dublin, then at a peak of intellectual and academic excellence. It is possible that Congreve's interest in the stage began, like Southerne's and Farquhar's, with visits to Dublin's Smock Alley Theatre;[2] but the Revolution of 1688 drove Congreve away to England, and he probably arrived in London about the middle of 1689, and entered the Middle Temple to read law in March 1691.[3]

Congreve soon gained the attention and affection of John Dryden, lately Poet Laureate and now sixty years old; his respect for Congreve's classical scholarship and creative talent resulted in the invitation to translate the eleventh satire in a collection of Juvenal published in 1692. In the same year Dryden published Congreve's commendatory verses as sole preface to his translation of Persius, Congreve himself brought out his short prose romance *Incognita*, and finally he showed the script of his first comedy, *The Old Bachelor*, to Dryden. With the recommendation of Dryden and Southerne it was acted at the Theatre Royal in 1693 with brilliant success. Congreve was twenty-three, and claimed to have written the play even earlier, presumably during his first year at the Middle Temple.[4] He dedicated it to Charles Boyle, whose Irish estates Congreve's father had begun to manage in 1690; the gesture is characteristic of Congreve in its combination of filial piety, judicious worldliness, and social grace.

[1] Biographical facts are taken from John C. Hodges, *William Congreve : Letters and Documents* (London, 1964).

[2] For an account of the Smock Alley Theatre see W. S. Clark, *The Early Irish Stage* (Oxford, 1955). [3] Hodges, op. cit., p. 89.

[4] For discussion of this question see the present writer's 'Congreve's *The Old Bachelor* and Jonsonian Comedy' in *William Congreve*, Mermaid Critical Commentaries (London, 1972).

In the same year, 1693, his second comedy *The Double Dealer* had a disappointing reception at the Theatre Royal. Dryden lent powerful support by contributing a verse commendation published with the play, and Congreve, in the dedication, angrily refuted hostile criticism based, as he maintained, on misapprehension of the comic mode of the play. However, there is a weakness in its melodramatic portrayals of villainy and innocence which betrays the uncertainly controlled influence of the Jacobean dramatist John Fletcher, even though the play marks a key stage in Congreve's artistic development: it is his first attempt to develop a comic mode which can incorporate serious human experience without discarding the essential richness of the inherited comic tradition.

From this point of view, Congreve's next play, *Love for Love* (1695), appears to confirm his early gift for conventional gay comedy, rather than to present a further development of the mode of *The Double Dealer*. Yet *Love for Love* was a success, it gave Congreve fame and reputation, and amply rewarded Dryden for his faithful support of the young dramatist. Moreover, the play does certainly exhibit a new richness in characterisation, where frequent debts to Shakespeare, as well as Ben Jonson, are apparent.

In the same year, 1695, Congreve wrote the letter to Dennis concerning humour in comedy, which though not itself an important critical essay is a confirmation of the deep agreement in matters of principle between Dryden and Congreve, not merely as friends, but as creative artists. Congreve shared Dryden's convictions, especially in his emphasis on Ben Jonson as a model for comic writers, his admiration for the Roman playwright Terence, and his faith in the supreme genius of the English for comedy, while Dryden looked to the young Congreve to fulfil the ideal set forth in his essay *Of Dramatic Poesy*, that an English comic dramatist should learn from the genius in characterisation of Shakespeare, the correctness and strength in design of Jonson, the gaiety in spirit of Fletcher, and the polish and grace in dialogue of Dryden's own age. When Congreve, in dedicating *The Way of the World* to Montague, attributed the quality of its dialogue to his experience of the earl's conversation, the explicit compliment to Montague was also therefore an implicit homage to Dryden; in addition, Congreve probably recalled that Dryden had paid exactly the same compliment to the Earl of Rochester in the dedication of *Marriage à la Mode* in 1672.

Congreve, in the dedication to Montague, had compared his patronage to that which Scipio and Laelius afforded Terence. This is really much more than an agreeably civilised classical allusion; it is characteristic of Congreve's graceful and truly witty scholarship, for the comparison holds fully, and implies much about Congreve's attitude to his own career.

Terence,[5] who commanded the profound respect of Ben Jonson and of Dryden, is famous for his development of the Greek comedy of Menander, for the subtlety and elegance of his dialogue and characterisation, for his introduction of double-plots and complex romantic intrigues in place of the lively farcical manner of his predecessor Plautus, and for a career brief, brilliant, and controversial. Like Congreve, Terence wrote his first play at twenty-one; he read it to an elderly Roman dramatist, who admired it, and the play had a brilliant stage success. Terence won entry into the best social and intellectual circle in the capital, where he found defenders and patrons, but he suffered on occasion from the bad taste of audiences who, disappointed by the absence of farce in his *Hecyra*, turned away to the rival attractions of tightrope walkers, boxers, and gladiators. Congreve could find here obvious analogies to the taste which rejected *The Double Dealer* and preferred such crude comedies as *Love and a Bottle* to *The Way of the World*. Even more exact, moreover, was the parallel between Collier's attack on Congreve and the persecution of Terence by an old playwright Luscius Lanuvinus, who plagued him with accusations of having contaminated his Greek sources, and remained obstinately blind to Terence's true concern, the creation of a subtler comic mode which substituted complexity in character and situation for the caricature and farce of the preceding age.

Congreve had been grateful for the defence which his friend Dryden's authority had afforded, when *The Double Dealer* was attacked; but four years later, when Congreve became one of Jeremy Collier's targets in the notorious *A Short View of The Immorality and Profaneness of the English Stage*, he replied with his own *Amendments of Mr Collier's False and Imperfect Citations*, no doubt fully conscious of the ironic parallel between the Roman and Puritan English meanings of 'contamination'.[6]

In his *Amendments*, Congreve argues with a lawyer's skill and a dramatist's spontaneous wit and immediacy of effect. His performance begins by playfully reversing Collier's images of dirt on to

[5] Details of Terence's career are taken from W. Beare, *The Roman Stage* (London, 1964).

[6] Lanuvinus used 'contaminatio', apparently, in the sense of *spoil* not *soil* or *pollute*; he was arguing that Terence was not producing faithful versions of Greek comedy but, by using several plays as the basis for a single play of his own, he was spoiling his inheritance; Jeremy Collier, on the other hand, accused Congreve of polluting the English stage with profaneness and immorality.

Collier's own head. Collier becomes for Congreve 'the evil Spirit', the thing of darkness, who has 'blackned the Thoughts with his own *Smut*', and therefore, declares Congreve, 'for his *Foot pads*, which he calls us in his Preface, and for his *Buffoons* . . . I will onely call him Mr. *Collier*'.[7] The tone is sprightly here, though it later becomes indignant. It has been suggested that Collier's attack made an impression on Congreve which resulted in the greater seriousness of theme in *The Way of the World*. It is true that Congreve's defence of the hero of *Love for Love*, Valentine, against Collier, adopts a sobriety of tone and attitude which is not really appropriate to the atmosphere of the play; Congreve declares 'the Character is a mix'd Character; his Faults are fewer than his good Qualities; and, as the World goes, he may pass well enough for the best Character in a Comedy; where even the best must be shewn to have Faults, that the best Spectators may be warn'd not to think too well of themselves'.[8]

The comment is interesting, particularly the phrase 'as the World goes', for if it seems unsuited to *Love for Love* it certainly is appropriate for the comedy which Congreve was actually composing at the time, *The Way of the World*, which first appeared at Lincoln's Inn Fields Theatre the following March, 1700.

It is evident from the substance of Congreve's dedication of this last comedy that he considered it his masterpiece, while his tone seems valedictory, implying his state of mind after the disappointing public reception of the play. If he were to cease writing comedy now, at the age of thirty, he would leave a complete if small oeuvre; there was critical controversy about its value, but he was confident that it met the highest classical standards; and there was also something extraordinary and compelling about the detailed coincidence between his own career and his venerated predecessors, Terence and Ben Jonson. Each of them had forged a new comic form, meeting controversy and proudly defying it in declamatory prefaces and prologues, appealing to the authority of classical precept and example, and achieving great reputations in posterity. Congreve's classical temper and his extraordinary sensitivity to pattern must have been attracted by the idea of a retirement from comedy which would complete the parallel between himself, now thirty, and Terence, who left Rome at twenty-five after writing six comedies. Such an act, furthermore, would repeat the design of Ben Jonson's career, for he had been driven to temporary retirement after the

[7] Quotations from Congreve's *Amendments* are taken from Montague Summers, ed., *The Works of William Congreve* (London, 1923), III, 171–206.

[8] ibid., p. 200.

failure of *Catiline* by his contempt for the audience, and had proudly expressed his defiance in the *Ode to Himselfe*:[9]

> Come leave the loathed Stage,
> And the more loathsome Age,
> Where pride and impudence in faction knit,
> Usurpe the Chaire of wit:

Later in 1700 came the death of Dryden, and perhaps it was then that Congreve, with his extraordinary feeling for completed pattern, recognised in his own life the fulfilment of a design that rivalled art.

The relationship between Congreve's life and art seems to have been unusually and interestingly reciprocal, and we are not free to neglect Congreve's personal experience of the society of his time; dramatic comedy is, in any case, the most socially articulate form of the supremely social art of theatre, and there is point in weighing up the question. When Congreve came to London he was not rich. His favourable start was the result of his personal charm and his wit as much as his literary talent. He won entry to the select society of Dryden and the literary figures at Will's coffee house in Covent Garden, and this in turn led to entry into other circles: on one hand the society of the theatre, on the other of aristocrats like the Earl of Montague. Congreve's easy, graceful manners and gentlemanly tastes gained him the friendship and esteem of the famous and the great, but his career depended upon their influence and patronage, and he was obliged to handle his own modest means prudently and astutely for many years before he became at last rich. His early work displays an inclination to fantasy and absurdity, which give it great charm, but he was at the same time a student of law: his plays are plotted with strict and detailed precision, they deal with the manipulation of law to reconcile individual needs to social obligations, and they show the complex interweaving of relationships—of friendship, family, and business—in the select and intricate, polite metropolitan world.

In his personal affairs Congreve seems to have shown the judgement, tact, and humane good humour which characterise Mirabell himself. Dryden invited the legally knowledgeable Congreve to draw up his contracts with the publisher Jacob Tonson. The contract Congreve drew up for Dryden's *Virgil* was, it has been said, 'a shrewder document than one might expect from the poet';[10] evidently, however, Congreve matched legal acumen with tact.

[9] All quotations from Jonson taken from *Ben Jonson*, ed. C. H. Herford and P. and E. Simpson (Oxford, 1925–52).

[10] Hodges, op. cit., p. 76, points out that Congreve had been reading law for more than three years when this contract was drawn up.

He helped his friend Dryden, but his relationship with Tonson continued in later years to their mutual benefit, after Congreve had ceased to write and Dryden had died, for Tonson invited Congreve to join the Kit-Cat Club, founded about 1700 and including among its early members Steele, Walsh, Addison, Vanbrugh, and the Earl of Montague to whom Congreve had dedicated *The Way of the World*. Later, the Whig inclination of the Kit-Cat Club helped Congreve obtain the post of Secretary of Jamaica, and with prudent management of his lucrative salary Congreve amassed the fortune of ten thousand pounds.

This fortune became the focus of the memorable last act of his life. Congreve's attachment to Anne Bracegirdle had ceased, and in his last years he became the lover of the young Duchess of Marlborough. When her daughter Mary Godolphin was born in 1723 there was gossip that Congreve was the father, but most of this was forgotten when it developed that Congreve's will named the duchess' husband as executor, and it came to be accepted that the relationship had been platonic. In his will Congreve had first made the duchess executrix, then, no doubt with the aim of avoiding gossip or scandal, named her husband in her place. His true motives can only be understood by considering the interlocking will of the duchess, not written until four years later and not made public. Her will required that her body be buried not at Blenheim but in Westminster Abbey, near the Earl of Godolphin, that is, in the same part of the abbey as she had buried Congreve. Furthermore, her will dealt chiefly with her daughter Mary, to whom she specifically left 'all Mr Congreves Personal Estate that he left me', plate engraved 'with Mr Congreves Armes', three thousand pounds, and jewels worth seven thousand five hundred pounds purchased with the money Congreve left her. So, as John C. Hodges explains,[11]

> If Mary Godolphin was his daughter, he naturally wanted her to have his personal things, his plate engraved with the Congreve arms and the choice collection of books he valued so highly. And all this he wanted to pass along quietly, without scandal or embarrassment. He would hardly have considered naming Mary directly as his heir. To do so would multiply gossip without end. He could depend on the mother, as sole executrix, to care for his property and pass it along in her will to Mary. But on second thought, Congreve apparently realized that he could accomplish his purpose regarding his property and at the same time help to quiet gossip by naming the husband of the Duchess as his sole executor. The will, it should be noted, was carefully drawn to restrict the powers of the husband and to leave the Duchess entirely free to transmit Congreve's property (as she did) to Mary.

[11] ibid., p. 251.

Here Congreve achieved in his own life an 'artful solution of the fable', and contrived a plot which worked through the manipulation of law and the conveyance of an estate in trust, to achieve the essential resolution of comedy, 'an individual release which is also a social reconciliation'.[12]

THE PLAY

The titles of Congreve's successive comedies suggest a steady development and a concern with progressively wider areas of experience, beginning with the relatively limited scope of *The Old Bachelor* and concluding with that more comprehensive theme, *The Way of the World*. However, the maturity and range of Congreve's comedy are relative to the theatrical conditions which prevailed and to the actors who interpreted his roles, as well as to the strictly limiting conventions within which he wrote. Congreve practised a classical economy in stagecraft; he designed all his plots around the conventional set of comic roles, and accepted themes, of the comedy of manners; moreover, his four comedies were presented within a period of only seven years, at two theatres, the Theatre Royal and the Lincoln's Inn Fields Theatre, which differed only in the inferior size and condition of the latter.[13] *Love for Love*, in fact, had been 'read and accepted of at the Theatre Royal',[14] but Congreve withheld it during the dispute which led to Betterton's move to Lincoln's Inn Fields, where the play was then performed. In due course *The Mourning Bride* (Congreve's tragedy) and *The Way of the World* were performed there also.

This close continuity, which is so important an element in Congreve's plays, was further strengthened by the remarkably select number of actors who created the successive major roles. The same actor, Betterton, created Heartwell, Maskwell, Valentine, Osmyn, and Fainall; the same actress, Mrs Bracegirdle, created all Congreve's heroines from Araminta to Millamant; indeed only one major actor in *The Way of the World*, John Verbruggen, had not been in at least two of Congreve's previous comedies, and even he had once understudied Williams, the original Vainlove and Mellefont.

[12] Northrop Frye, 'The Argument of Comedy' in A. Nicoll, *The Theatre and Dramatic Theory* (London, 1962), p. 125.

[13] Cibber describes it at the time it was closed as 'but small, and poorly fitted up within the Walls of a Tennis *Quaree* Court, which is of the lesser sort': *An Apology for the Life of Mr Colley Cibber* (new ed. London, 1889), I,314–15.

[14] ibid., I, 197.

What is more, these were the most distinguished actors of the time: Betterton, the greatest Shakespearean actor between Burbage and Garrick; Mrs Barry, the most celebrated actress of the Restoration, famous for her tragic roles (Cibber:[15] 'In Scenes of Anger, Defiance, or Resentment, while she was impetuous and terrible, she pour'd out the Sentiment with an enchanting Harmony') but also the original Mrs Loveit in Etherege's masterpiece *The Man of Mode*. Having seen Mrs Barry's Lady Touchwood in *The Double Dealer*, Congreve doubtless had a compelling reason for his continuing preoccupation with a more serious mode of comedy.

Among the comic roles a similar pattern is evident. Sir Wilfull was created by Underhill, a noted Gravedigger in *Hamlet*, and successful not only as Sir Sampson in *Love for Love* but in such buffoon roles as Justice Clodpate, Sir Nobel Clumsey, Lolpoop, Oldwit, and so on;[16] while Mrs Leigh, who created Lady Wishfort, had years before created the original of the part, Lady Woodvil in *The Man of Mode*. As for the heroine, Anne Bracegirdle, she was according to Cibber the darling of the theatre, and 'when she acted *Millamant* all the Faults, Follies, and Affectations of that agreeable Tyrant were venially melted down into so many Charms and Attractions of a conscious Beauty'.[17] It is said that Congreve was in love with Anne Bracegirdle, and Cibber retails the gossip that when Congreve gave her a lover in a play he seemed palpably to plead his own passion. Certainly the cumulative effect on the young dramatist of association with such gifted performers must have been richly rewarding, and for Congreve to see his plays interpreted by great actors must have been an educative experience, and no doubt contributed to the remarkable evolution of his art towards the mature assurance of his last comedy. It was his fortune to inherit a tradition which was supremely alive.

Congreve's talent for the creation of subtle characters and dialogue achieved full expression through actors of this high calibre; and in the stage conditions also his art found fulfilment. Here is Cibber again:

> the usual Station of the Actors, in almost every Scene, was advanc'd at least ten Foot nearer to the Audience than they now can be . . . But when the Actors were in Possession of that forwarder Space to advance upon, the Voice was then more in the Centre of the House, so that the most distant Ear had scarce the least Doubt or Difficulty in hearing what fell from the weakest Utterance: All Objects were thus drawn nearer to the Sense; every painted Scene was stronger . . . every rich or fine-coloured Habit had a more lively Lustre.[18]

[15] ibid., I, 160.
[16] ibid., I, 154–5.
[17] ibid., I, 173.
[18] ibid., II, 85.

The actors in this forward area played in front of painted flats running in grooves within the proscenium arch and closing together in the centre of the stage; if scenery or properties were needed in the scene, these flats parted to disclose the inner stage.[19]

In *The Way of the World* all the action is designed to be played in the forward area except for the initial discovery of Fainall and Mirabell seated at cards in Act I, and for the perambulations in the park in Act II, where both the forward and inner stages were probably used, with the park scene represented by painted flats, and possibly also 'relieves', that is scenes in relief, moulded scenes, and cut scenes where part of the flat was cut out to show a distant prospect extending behind. For the rest, Congreve's requirements in painted scenes were simple and formal: flats drawn across to represent the room in Lady Wishfort's house, and the room in the chocolate-house. Congreve's requirements may be seen as a conscious reflection of the special sense of 'the world' when it means polite metropolitan society with its rigid, formalised, and interchangeable façades, limited in number, providing the flat background against which the characters, so contrastingly full of animation, depth, and movement, act in tension.

So, when the curtain draws for Act I, it discovers a conventional theatrical tableau: two gamesters at cards in a chocolate-house. As they rise and begin to converse, the card-game dissolves to become a metaphor for the dramatic action, and the two men, at first sight so similar, begin to acquire particular and very different identities.

The process is gradual; Congreve's exposition is indirect, much of it conveyed by inference, for in this play it is at least as important to establish the fluidity and uncertainty of the atmosphere as it is to indicate the pattern of characters and plot. In the opening dialogue there is a subtle instability of tone; the hints, evasions, and insinuations convey the impression of much being withheld; and precisely this impression is necessary to a proper understanding of the play, which is concerned to bring this intricate texture, the texture of real life in society, into focus with the traditional ideals of comedy. Congreve's purpose is to find a means of reconciling the ideals of moral conduct with the actualities of social experience at the time; in short, it is an endeavour to modify the art of comedy to make its morality more inclusive and reconciliatory, less ideal and remote.

Congreve begins the play by emphasising the similarity between the situation of Mirabell and that of Fainall, but as the action develops it becomes clear that there is a crucial distinction between them, and this is made explicit in the last scene when Mirabell,

[19] See Montague Summers, *The Restoration Theatre* (London, 1934).

having beaten Fainall at his own game, flings back at Fainall the cheap and base cynicism which has guided his embittered career in the play; for when Mirabell taunts him with the phrase 'the way of the world' [20] the audience will recall Fainall's use of it, first when reassuring his mistress Mrs Marwood that he loves her and would be rid of his wife, and has 'something of a constitution to bustle through the ways of wedlock and this world',[21] and the second time, when he learns of her adultery, he reflects bitterly that their doubly adulterous marriage is 'in the way of the world'.[22] Mirabell, however, lives differently, according to another interpretation of the phrase; and it is in Mirabell that Congreve exhibits his own ideal of virtuous action, something with which he was preoccupied at the time he wrote the play, to judge from his account of Valentine's career in *Love for Love*: 'he has honesty enough to close with a hard Bargain, rather than not pay his Debts, in the first *Act*; and he has Generosity and Sincerity enough, in the last *Act*, to sacrifice every thing to his Love; and when he is in danger of losing his Mistress, thinks every thing else of little worth'.[23] If we add to this the remark already quoted, that 'as the World goes, he may pass well enough for the best Character in a Comedy; where even the best must be shewn to have Faults, that the best Spectators may be warn'd not to think too well of themselves', Congreve's emphasis on Mirabell's prodigal past, and present dependence on the goodwill of Mrs Fainall, his ex-mistress, and Lady Wishfort, Millamant's aunt, becomes comprehensible. Underlying the comic action is the romantic theme of the hero proving his worth and winning the hand of the fair heroine; but the contrast between the situation of Mirabell and that of his Shakespearean ancestor Benedick is clear when we notice how complex and sophisticated – and prosaic – Mirabell's task is, where Benedick has but to challenge Claudio and refute Beatrice's charge that

> manhood is melted into curtsies, valour into compliment, and men are only turned into tongue, and trim ones too; (*Much Ado*, IV, i)

Benedick has courage, gaiety, hope untarnished by experience; such spirit informs the exchange between the lovers in *The Double Dealer* as Cynthia banters with Mellefont:[24]

> 'Tis an odd game we're going to play at: What think you of drawing Stakes

[20] V, 501. [21] II, 188–9. [22] III, 547.
[23] *Amendments*, ed.cit., III, 200.
[24] Quotations from other plays of Congreve taken from Herbert Davis, ed., *The Complete Plays of William Congreve* (Chicago and London, 1967).

Mellefont answers from the heart without denying his youthful inexperience; his response has hope, not wisdom, it has the strength that comes of immaturity:

> No, hang't, that's not endeavouring to Win, because it's possible we may lose; since we have Shuffled and Cutt, let's e'en turn up Trump now. (II, 157–61)

With the opening of *The Way of the World*, imagery from cards offers itself as the natural way of describing the behaviour of Mirabell and Fainall, but the mood is very far from the gaiety of Mellefont and Cynthia, as each man seeks to elicit information from the other without revealing his own hand. The shifting texture of their conversation reflects their awareness of the complexity of the case, and if each man's motives become clearer as fragments of information emerge, there is still much that the audience does not know when the dialogue ends. The chief cause of tension between them is Mrs Marwood. She has frustrated the plan of Mirabell to gain Lady Wishfort's approval of his match with Millamant. Mirabell suspects Fainall of being Mrs Marwood's lover and privy to her designs; in his turn Fainall suspects her of being attracted to Mirabell (one reason why she frustrated the match, perhaps), so he seeks to establish whether Mirabell returns the sentiment or not.

When Fainall makes the jesting remark to Mirabell that he would not make love to a woman who undervalued the loss of her reputation, each of them at once thinks of the other's relationship to Mrs Marwood. Mirabell replies

> You have a taste extremely delicate, and are for refining on your pleasures. (I, 10–11)

This is both an evasion of the proffered subject and a coolly ironic reproof of Fainall's libertine wit. Fainall counters by interpreting this reproof as merely a sign of ill-humour, and hints that he suspects the cause to be a woman. Mirabell denies it lightly, and Fainall reacts to the change in tone at once with his more bantering remarks about Millamant. Mirabell, instead of relaxing his guard, pursues this subject for some time, preserving the playful tone to fend off Fainall's leading questions and indirect insinuations without quite dropping the question of Mrs Marwood. Fainall becomes less oblique as his frustration increases, and much of his character is revealed in his choice of phrase:

> The discovery of your sham addresses to her, to conceal your love to her neice, has provoked this separation. Had you dissembled better, things might have continued in the state of nature. (I, 59–62)

Mirabell neutralises the innuendo by resorting to playful nonsense about Lady Wishfort, then suddenly insinuates that Fainall is Mrs Marwood's lover. The quick reaction this provokes possibly suggests Fainall's guilt; certainly Mirabell's tone becomes more cool as he allows Fainall a glimpse of his private, contemptuous opinion of him:

> one of those coxcombs who are apt to interpret a woman's good manners to her prejudice

and then trumps Fainall's last bid:

> FAINALL
> ... Yet you speak with an indifference which seems to be affected, and confesses you are conscious of a negligence.
> MIRABELL
> You pursue the argument with a distrust that seems to be unaffected, and confesses you are conscious of a concern, for which the lady is more indebted to you than your wife.
> (I, 85–90)

Mirabell fastidiously reorders Fainall's own phrases to make a penetrating judgement; Fainall does not reply, but makes a tactical withdrawal under the pressure of Mirabell's firm authority.

Now, it is sometimes argued that from a first reading of this conversation between Mirabell and Fainall, one might suppose there was no difference between the two men: that there is a tendency to coalescence in the dialogue.[25] This is unlikely to be a problem in the theatre, where actors will make provisional distinctions possible very early, but in any case a second encounter follows almost at once, and there the two men are clearly contrasted in their attitudes to love and marriage, in their feelings of generosity and cynicism. What is implicit, tentatively and subtly discernible, in the first encounter, becomes gradually explicit and clear. The initial obscurity is important, too: as the exposition unfolds in Acts I and II, the audience's understanding of Mirabell, and admiration for him, will evolve, but not without hesitations: 'even the best must be shewn to have Faults': and as a consequence Congreve's concern with conduct *in society* will come into clear focus.

In the dedication of *The Way of the World* Congreve wrote that his concern was with characters of affected wit: 'a wit, which at the same time that it is affected, is also false'. Fainall's falsity is deter-

[25] This point is made by Ian Donaldson, *The World Upside Down* (Oxford, 1970), p. 125. I cannot agree with him that Congreve's moral design in the play is insufficiently fastidious as a consequence of its narrative subtlety; rather I find the subtlety contributes to the moral fastidiousness of the design.

mined, forceful, and menacing later in the action, of course, but it is suggested with subtlety and consistency from the outset. So clear, indeed, is the logic of Congreve's exposition that details of the Mirabell-Fainall relationship not revealed until Act II help to explain, retrospectively, some of the tensions in the first conversation in the play. The essential distinction between Mirabell and Fainall – which must be a dominant concern – is in fidelity to genuine convictions, integrity, and generosity of feeling. Indeed, such is the superficial elegance and social awareness of Mirabell's discourse that it may be worth emphasising the strength and energy of his emotions; as Bonamy Dobrée[26] has well remarked, 'Not to see this passionate side of Congreve is to lose the best in him; it is like reading Shakespeare to find that he does not conform to classical rules'. Fainall's similarity to Mirabell is confined to the superficial facility in phrasing, the practised control of entertaining anecdote, malicious innuendo, and quickness in repartee, common to everyone in society, including, as Congreve takes pains to emphasise, such fools as Witwoud and Petulant.

This is not to say, of course, that there are not differences of degree among false wits in the play. On the contrary, there is a strict hierarchy, from Fainall – played by Betterton, and not a comic part – to Witwoud and thence to Petulant, who is nearly all vapour, and tends as a consequence to be explosive (so betraying his Elizabethan lineage).[27] This hierarchy of false wit is indicated by the order in which characters appear in Act I, so that the audience has the opportunity to measure each in turn against Mirabell, the true wit, and to compare relative degrees of folly. This gradual exposition is accompanied by successive moods, each more free than the last; in this way the transition is effected from the still tense mood of Fainall's second dialogue with Mirabell to the frankly farcical entrance of Petulant at the end of the Act.

The modulation from the opening mood to the freer comedy of Witwoud is effected in this second dialogue of Mirabell and Fainall, where Congreve succeeds in preserving the complex texture of their relationship while allowing the true spirit of comedy release. Fainall introduces once more the subject of Millamant, and, seeking to be both agreeable and amusing, remarks that she has wit. Mirabell's reply affects an even tone, but is full of feeling and warmth:

[26] *Restoration Comedy 1660–1720* (London, 1924), p. 146.

[27] There are echoes of Falstaff, Pistol, and even Corporal Nym in Petulant's speech—compare Petulant's threat of throat-cutting soon after his entrance in Act I with the similar threat of Nym (*Henry V*, II, i, 20–25, in *The Complete Works of Shakespeare*, ed. Peter Alexander (London, 1951)). Petulant is chiefly derived from Jonson's obstreperous fools, of course.

She has beauty enough to make any man think so, and complaisance enough not to contradict him who shall tell her so. (I, 137–8)

But Fainall has little taste for this, and deflects the conversation back to repartee. Mirabell, whose feelings are now aroused, cannot be diverted, and embarks on a fuller declaration of his love for Millamant and a fine expression of his generosity of spirit, which even sweetens the potentially cynical figure of paradox:

I like her with all her faults, nay, like her for her faults. (I,142–3)

Fainall responds with the curt, bitter, and revealing comment that marriage changes all that:

Ay, ay, I have experience: I have a wife, and so forth. (I, 161)

The bitterness of Fainall is limiting and distorting, whereas the warmth and generosity of Mirabell widen the range and enrich the quality of his experience, and his speech.

Part of Mirabell's preoccupation, when conversing with Fainall, is in gauging Fainall's relationship with Mrs Fainall. In Act I we cannot know this, though we can detect Mirabell's implicitly reproving attitude to Fainall's cynical dismissal of his marriage. However, Mirabell has good reason for concern at Fainall's evident alienation from his wife, as the second Act reveals; and it is here that Congreve's concern with a more inclusively realistic drama is apparent. The scene between Mirabell and Mrs Fainall[28] is preceded by the passionate and painful encounter of Mrs Marwood and Fainall in which accusations and counter-accusations, alternating with gestures of defiance and conciliation, exhibit the essentially selfish quality of their feelings and the corrosive effects of the liaison:

MRS. MARWOOD
'Tis false, you urged it with deliberate malice—'twas spoke in scorn, and I never will forgive it.
FAINALL
Your guilt, not your resentment, begets your rage. If yet you loved, you could forgive a jealousy; but you are stung to find you are discovered. (II, 158–62)

The contrast between this and the scene which immediately follows between Mirabell and Mrs Fainall is deliberate, exact, and significant. First we are shown Mrs Marwood with her partner in adultery (Fainall); then Mrs Fainall with her erstwhile lover (Mirabell). Although both men defend themselves by arguing that they have preserved reputations,[29] they do so in contrasting ways

[28] II, 222–85. [29] II, 173, 234.

which reveal much: Mirabell's admission is not evasive or aggressive, but gentle and reasonable as well as frank and complete; he brings out Mrs Fainall's latent generosity by reminding her of the truth of their past relationship, dissolving the bitterness she seemed to declare (with whatever disingenuous motives) to Mrs Marwood at the beginning of the Act. It is true that Mirabell knows he can win over Mrs Fainall because she still feels affection for him; on the other hand she does not resist his firm, implicit assumption that their relationship could never have ended in marriage. Mirabell admits his own culpability in a disagreeable affair; on the other hand he reminds Mrs Fainall of her equal responsibility in the phrase '*our* loves'. Mirabell shows Mrs Fainall the hollowness of the worldly wisdom she had exchanged with Mrs Marwood;[30] he has ceased to love her, but does not loathe her. Of course, at the same time, Mirabell's judgement of her is shrewd, and is confirmed by her acceptance of a future in which, secured (by his foresight) from the menace of Fainall, she can adopt the programme suggested by Mrs Marwood, and not refuse the sweets of life because they once must leave her, although in her heart she knows that one day she will be old, and fit only for the part of Lady Wishfort, withering in an affected bloom. Mrs Fainall is in these terms an affected wit, a false wit; but her assent to Mirabell's wishes indicates her recognition of his truth, and is the key to the ultimate success of Mirabell's endeavour to win the favour of Lady Wishfort herself. Congreve stresses that Mirabell has had experience, his maturity has been bought with a knowledge of suffering and a degree of guilt; but like Valentine in *Love for Love* he is generous, and is rewarded by the generosity of Mrs Fainall; in this sense it is possible to see Mirabell's career in the play as a demonstration of his reformation, closely contrasted to the degeneration of his opponent Fainall, and echoed by the natures of their respective mistresses, Mrs Marwood and Mrs Fainall.[31] This indicates little more than a crude outline, of course, since the centre of the design is Millamant. Mirabell's past experience of the disagreeable aspects of the World matters most because it has educated him to a mature awareness of the need for prudence, judiciousness, tolerance, and a shrewd insight into the base motives which men are heir to; without all this, generosity would aid Mirabell no more than it does Sir Wilfull, who has quantities of the spirit, in a raw condition, but who appears to Millamant, and even to Lady Wishfort, repellent.

Millamant's arrival completes Congreve's design of the Act; the

[30] II, 1–24.

[31] This is the central argument of Paul and Miriam Mueschke, *A New View of Congreve's Way of the World* (Michigan, 1958).

encounter between the bitter couple, Fainall and Mrs Marwood, is succeeded by that between the forgiving ex-lovers Mirabell and Mrs Fainall, and that in turn precedes the meeting of the witty, loving couple Mirabell and Millamant who will marry, and who embody the play's ideals. Millamant has more gaiety than Mirabell ('Sententious Mirabell! Prithee don't look with that violent and inflexible wise face') and indeed her entrance releases the comic spirit which has been hitherto suppressed in Act II. Congreve's genius in characterisation extends to the gayer characters; Millamant is impish, she deliberately exaggerates her affectations to provoke Mirabell, using the presence of Witwoud and Mincing to elude his efforts and to fill the stage with airy vitality; Mirabell reacts by exaggerating his own truly valuable capacity for seriousness, and like Rosalind Millamant instantly seizes on his slight falsity of tone, his dull apprehension of the mood:

> . . . Beauty the lover's gift! Lord, what is a lover, that it can give? Why, one makes lovers as fast as one pleases, and they live as long as one pleases, and they die as soon as one pleases; and then, if one pleases, one makes more. (II, 360–63)

Millamant is really in love, like Rosalind in *As You Like It*; and though she does not declare that her affection 'hath an unknown bottom, like the Bay of Portugal'[32] the whole effect of her performance depends upon the audience's recognition of the fact, so that it shares the joke against Mirabell and the secret joy of Millamant's possession of the experience. The audience will side with Millamant also over the matter of her tolerance of the herd of fools, recognising the element of jealousy in Mirabell's objection but also confident that Millamant is his equal in judgement, as she tantalises him with her wit. When she leaves him, the comic atmosphere has become so free and auspicious that he bursts out with a passionate exclamation:

> Think of you! To think of a whirlwind, though 'twere in a whirlwind, were a case of more steady contemplation: (II, 437–9)

The speech, as the images make plain, has a truly powerful intensity of feeling, the feeling which has been present throughout the scene with Millamant, which underlies all their witty exchanges. The point is crucial. They are not anaemic, a fop and a coquette, though they have breeding, wit, and tact; they are man and woman, and the major scenes of the play – involving Fainall and Mrs Marwood as well as Mirabell and Millamant – are passionate and powerful.

This fact is emphasised by the sharp contrast with the absurdity

[32] *As You Like It*, IV, i, 187–8.

of the postures Lady Wishfort adopts, with desperate yet unflagging energy; she has a Jonsonian ability to inflate herself into a simulacrum of a romantic heroine, but she remains a sort of female Epicure Mammon in her hopes, and a Volpone in her looks:

> Let me see the glass. Cracks, sayest thou? Why, I am arrantly flayed! I look like an old peeled wall! Thou must repair me Foible, before Sir Rowland comes . . . (III, 130–3)

Congreve's rich inheritance from Shakespearean and Jonsonian comedy is generously spent in *The Way of the World;* for if the grand strokes of caricature proclaim the influence of Jonson, the marvellously particular and complete identities of the comic characters owe much to Shakespeare's example. Lady Wishfort and Sir Wilfull can be moving as well as ridiculous, though the effect is momentary, like Sir Andrew Aguecheek in *Twelfth Night* melancholically confessing 'I was adored once too', or like Dogberry in *Much Ado* remembering that he has 'had losses'. Perhaps it is just these sad moments in the lives of the old (and mostly ridiculous) minor characters which bring them so completely to life, modifying the comic atmosphere from hilarity to a blend of melancholy so familiar elsewhere in the plays of Chekhov. In creating Lady Wishfort Congreve has drawn on the Nurse in *Romeo and Juliet*[33] as well as taking a full measure of the immediate original (created by Mrs Leigh), Lady Woodvil in *The Man of Mode*; but the poetic richness of Lady Wishfort's half-ridiculous, half-pitiable imposture of youth and outraged dignity owes something to Falstaff too:

> A cup! Save thee, and what a cup hast thou brought! Dost thou take me for a fairy, to drink out of an acorn? (III, 25–6)

Sir Wilfull's part in the finale recalls that of Kastril in Act IV of *The Alchemist*, but Sir Wilfull brings from Shropshire a loam-footed honesty and a speech as richly flavoured as a nut or an apple, which eventually win him some credit (he is given greater reward by Henry Fielding, who draws on him for Squire Western in *Tom Jones*). In the magnificent first encounter between Sir Wilfull and his half-brother Witwoud, haunting echoes of Falstaff and Justice Shallow enrich the atmosphere as Sir Wilfull discloses that Witwoud 'lived with honest Pumplenose the attorney of Furnival's Inn';[34]

[33] Compare *Romeo and Juliet*, II, v, 147–51: 'Scurvy knave! I am none of his flirt-gills; I am none of his skains-mates. And thou must stand by too, and suffer every knave to use me at his pleasure?' with Lady Wishfort's 'Audacious villain! Handle me! Would he durst! Frippery! Old frippery! Was there ever such a foul-mouthed fellow?'

[34] See *2 Henry IV*, III, ii, 13–14: 'I was once of Clement's Inn; where I think they will talk of mad Shallow yet.'

Falstaffian images occur to Witwoud in observing that Sir Wilfull's foreign tour will make him 'refined, like a Dutch skipper from a whale-fishing'. It is perhaps inevitable, as well as appropriate and traditional, that the hilarious scene of intoxication in Act IV (always the farcical climax in Jonsonian comedy) should be dominated by this embodiment of instinct and appetite, vital, anarchic, close to the well-springs of the comic spirit, including fragments of Sir Toby Belch's memorable performance[35] of drunken caterwauling, making 'an alehouse of my lady's house'.

Sir Wilfull's earthy saturnalian revels meet with a reaction from Millamant which we may associate with her reaction to Mirabell's provisos for their marriage:

> MIRABELL
> . . . *Item*, when you shall be breeding—
> MILLAMANT
> Ah! Name it not.
> MIRABELL
> Which may be presumed, with a blessing on our endeavours—
> MILLAMANT
> Odious endeavours! (IV, 223–8)

Millamant, notwithstanding such affected attitudes, cannot withstand instinct and inclination; she seeks only to temper instinct with order, not to suppress it – and judging by Sir Wilfull's expression of instinct, there is no suppressing it anyway:

> MILLAMANT
> Your pardon madam, I can stay no longer – Sir Wilfull grows very powerful – egh! How he smells! I shall be overcome if I stay. Come, cousin.
> LADY WISHFORT
> Smells! He would poison a tallow chandler and his family. Beastly creature, I know not what to do with him. (IV, 376–80)

Lady Wishfort, of course, has never known how to reconcile the demands of human nature with the rules of society, vacillating always between attenuated politeness:

> I hope you do not think me prone to any iteration of nuptials. (IV, 464–5)

and grossly extravagant abuse:

> Go! Go! That I took from washing of old gauze and weaving of dead hair, with a bleak blue nose, over a chafing dish of starved embers, and dining behind a traverse rag, in a shop no bigger than a bird-cage. Go, go, starve again! Do! Do! (V, 3–7)

[35] *Twelfth Night*, II, iii.

Lady Wishfort never has balance, Millamant never loses it, not even at the moment of triumph:

> Why does not the man take me? Would you have me give myself to you over again? (V, 536–7)

Millamant's poise is ideal, she achieves personal fulfilment without infringing the laws of society; but the play as a whole shows that her fulfilment is dependent on the skill of Mirabell, and is achieved through confronting experience of a more serious and widely inclusive range than the conventions of comedy normally allow. If Congreve succeeds, in *The Way of the World*, in modifying the art of comedy to make its morality more inclusive and reconciliatory, less ideal and remote, he remains faithful to the spirit of romantic comedy in its central affirmation of the power of love: for the play shows how Mirabell imposes on the cynically realistic way of the world the more generous vision of the art of comedy. *The Way of the World* is not an ironic title, it is reconciliatory; properly understood, the play is a celebration.

THE SOURCES

An editor required to produce a complete account of the sources of *The Way of The World* might be forgiven for answering, with Benedick, that he would rather go on the slightest errand to the Antipodes, fetch a toothpicker from the farthest inch of Asia, or a hair off the Great Cham's beard. In this play Congreve has drawn on a great range of comedy, from Plautus and Terence to Etherege, Molière, Shadwell, and Southerne. The theme is indicated by the epigraph from Horace's second satire in his *Satires, I*, the fate of adulterers and the fears of a guilty woman for the loss of her reputation. This didactic intent draws attention to the debt to Jonsonian critical comedy – especially *The Devil Is An Ass* (1616), *Bartholomew Fair* (1614), and *The Silent Woman* (1609). In the first-named of these, Fitzdottrel is disposed to treat his wife unfairly and desert her; Wittipol causes Fitzdottrel to convey her estate to Wittipol's friend Manly, and hence reduces Fitzdottrel to a state of financial dependence on his wife, and effects a *modus vivendi* for all parties.[36] In the second play, the wedding licence in the black box is the means to an 'artful solution of the fable', like the casket in Plautus' *Cistellaria;* and in the third, *The Silent Woman*, Truewit warns Morose before his marriage that 'This, too, with whom you are to marry, may have made a conveyance of her virginity beforehand, as your wise widdowes doe of their states, before they marry' (II, ii, 140). Real-life instances of this situation in the Jacobean period have been recorded, to extend Congreve's possible sources to infinity.[37]

The debt to Jonson is a testimony to Congreve's classical and conservative inclination, since Jonson himself 'Englished' Roman and Greek comedy. In complex romantic intrigue and subtlety of character and dialogue Congreve is indebted, as he himself claims, to Terence, though Terence's plays are innocent of the didactic impulse which Horatian non-dramatic satire passed on to Jonson and hence to Congreve. There can be little doubt that the Horatian epigraph is intended as an indication of the critical element in the comedy, while the central figures Mirabell and Millamant originate in Benedick and Beatrice in *Much Ado About Nothing* as well as in

[36] See Kathleen Lynch, *The Social Mode of Restoration Comedy* (London, 1926), pp. 192–3.

[37] See L. G. Salingar, 'Farce and Fashion in *The Silent Woman*', *Essays and Studies* (London, 1967).

the many gay couples of earlier Restoration comedies.[38] The proviso scene had been invented by Honoré D'Urfé (*L'Astrée*, 1607–27) and Congreve borrows verbally from Dryden's *Secret Love* for the scene. There are other echoes of Dryden's *Marriage à la Mode* and *The Wild Gallant*, and there is a general debt in structure and style to Etherege's *The Man of Mode*, and Congreve even inherited two of the original actors of that play to perform similar roles in his own comedy. There are memories of Sir Toby Belch and Falstaff and other buffoons in Sir Wilfull, and also of Peregrine in Brome's comedy *The Antipodes*; Lady Wishfort is compounded of memories of Etherege's Lady Woodvil but also of Jonson (Morose, Volpone, Ursula, Face) and Shakespeare (the Nurse in *Romeo and Juliet*, Falstaff). Petulant derives from Jonsonian quarrellers and from Nym in *Henry IV*. There are perhaps debts to Shadwell; *Bury Fair* (1689) may have suggested Lady Wishfort's ridiculous education of her daughter,[39] though Molière's *L'École des Femmes* is a more obvious source, and *The Amorous Bigot* (1690) may have suggested the Sir Rowland episode – though this is a variation on the gulling of Malvolio, itself an ancient *lazzo*.

Like Congreve's earlier comedies, *The Way of the World* has a strictly formalised design and all its characters are types from the comedy of manners; what is more, Congreve's own plays provide the most important source for this last masterpiece, which evolves from them. It is a sign of his greater maturity here that the magisterial Shakespearean comic language is absorbed into the texture of his play without control being lost; and the use of Shakespearean and Jonsonian material here suggests the unattainable ideal to which Congreve aspired, and the essentially English character of his art.

[38] The fuller history of their ancestry is in J. H. Smith, *The Gay Couple in Restoration Comedy* (Cambridge, Mass., 1948).

[39] Kathleen Lynch, ed., *The Way of the World* (London, 1965), p. xiv.

* *

THE TEXT

The copy-text for this edition is the first quarto of 1700 in the British Museum. This has been collated with the second quarto of 1706 and the editions of 1710 and 1719. I have consulted the editions of Montague Summers (London, 1923), Kathleen Lynch (London, 1965), and Herbert Davis (London, 1967). Spelling and punctuation have been modernised. Textual notes are printed at the foot of the relevant page; *Q1* refers to the edition of 1700, *Q2* to that of 1706, *W1* to the collected edition of 1710, and *W2* to that of 1719; *Ww* indicates agreement between readings in the two editions of 1710 and 1719.

FURTHER READING

The following books and articles are suggested in addition to those already mentioned in the Introduction.

Eric Bentley, *The Life of the Drama* (London, 1965), especially the chapter on comedy.
Allardyce Nicoll, *A History of English Drama 1660–1900,* Vol. I (London, 1961).
E. L. Avery, *Congreve's Plays on the Eighteenth Century Stage* (New York, 1952).
N. N. Holland, *The First Modern Comedies* (Cambridge, Mass., 1959).
W. H. Van Voris, *The Cultivated Stance* (London, 1966).
eds. J. R. Brown and Bernard Harris, *Restoration Theatre,* Stratford-upon-Avon Studies 6 (London, 1965).
ed. John Loftis, *Restoration Drama,* Galaxy Books (New York, 1966).
ed. E. Miner, *Restoration Dramatists,* Twentieth Century Views (Englewood Cliffs, 1966).
Peter Holland, *The Ornament of Action* (Cambridge, 1979).
Jocelyn Powell, *Restoration Theatre Production* (London, 1984).

THE Way of the World, A COMEDY.

As it is ACTED AT THE Theatre in *Lincoln's-Inn-Fields*, BY His Majesty's Servants.

Written by Mr. *CONGREVE.*

Audire est Opera pretium, procedere recte
Qui mæchis non vultis—— Hor. Sat. 2. l. 1.
——*Metuat doti deprensa.*—— Ibid.

LONDON:
Printed for *Jacob Tonson*, within *Gray's-Inn-Gate* next *Gray's-Inn-Lane.* 1700.

To the Right Honourable
RALPH
Earl of MONTAGUE, &c.

MY LORD,

Whether the world will arraign me of vanity, or not, that I have presumed to dedicate this comedy to your Lordship, I am yet in doubt: though it may be it is some degree of vanity even to doubt of it. One who has at any time had the honour of your Lordship's conversation, cannot be supposed to think very meanly of that which he would prefer to your perusal; yet it were to incur the imputation of too much sufficiency, to pretend to such a merit as might abide the test of your Lordship's censure.

Whatever value may be wanting to this play while yet it is mine, will be sufficiently made up to it, when it is once become your Lordship's; and it is my security, that I cannot have overrated it more by my dedication than your Lordship will dignify it by your patronage.

That it succeeded on the stage, was almost beyond my expectation; for but little of it was prepared for that general taste which seems now to be predominant in the palates of our audience.

Those characters which are meant to be ridiculous in most of our comedies are of fools so gross, that in my humble opinion they should rather disturb than divert the well-natured and reflecting part of an audience; they are rather objects of charity

20 *ridiculous* Q1 (ridiculed Q2, Ww)

Dedication Ralph Earl of Montague. Ralph Montague (1638–1709) was created Earl in 1689, having actively supported the deposition of James II and the installing of William III, after a long and intricate political career; he became Duke of Montague in 1705. He made two fortunes by marriage, his second marriage in 1692 to the Duchess of Newcastle being notable for the fact that she was very insane indeed, and had vowed only to marry a crowned head. Montague consequently presented himself to her as the Emperor of China, and was accepted! Whether this remarkable circumstance was in Congreve's mind when devising the Sir Rowland episode in the present play must remain a matter for conjecture.

7 *prefer* offer 8 *sufficiency* ability

than contempt; and instead of moving our mirth, they ought very often to excite our compassion.

This reflection moved me to design some characters which should appear ridiculous, not so much through a natural folly (which is incorrigible, and therefore not proper for the stage) as through an affected wit: a wit, which at the same time that it is affected, is also false. As there is some difficulty in the formation of a character of this nature, so there is some hazard which attends the progress of its success upon the stage; for many come to a play so over-charged with criticism that they very often let fly their censure, when through their rashness they have mistaken their aim. This I had occasion lately to observe; for this play has been acted two or three days before some of these hasty judges could find the leisure to distinguish betwixt the character of a Witwoud and a Truewit.

I must beg your Lordship's pardon for this digression from the true course of this epistle; but that it may not seem altogether impertinent, I beg that I may plead the occasion of it, in part of that excuse of which I stand in need, for recommending this comedy to your protection. It is only by the countenance of your Lordship, and the *few* so qualified, that such who write with care and pains can hope to be distinguished; for the prostituted name of *poet* promiscuously levels all that bear it.

Terence, the most correct writer in the world, had a Scipio and a Laelius, if not to assist him, at least to support him in his

38 *a Witwoud and a Truewit.* Witwoud in *The Way of the World* exemplifies the absurdity of affectation, and the ridiculous pretension to intelligence and judgement, common to the fools in the play. Truewit in Ben Jonson's *The Silent Woman* perceives and exposes—though rather cruelly—the false values and perverse conduct of the misanthrope Morose. Though Truewit has intelligence, ingenuity, and understanding based on a scholarly education, and Dryden thought him the best of Jonson's characters of gentlemen, he also thought Truewit inferior in gallantry and civility to gentlemen of his own time, which Dryden held to be 'much more courtly' ('Defence of the Epilogue' in John Dryden, *Of Dramatic Poesy and other Critical Essays*, ed. G. Watson [London, 1962], I, 180). Pope, with unusual misjudgement, was to repeat the objection that Congreve's fools had too much wit:

> Observe how seldom ev'n the best succeed:
> Tell me if Congreve's Fools are Fools indeed?
> (*Imitations of Horace*, Ep. II, i, 287–8).

47–8 *a Scipio and a Laelius.* Terence's patrons, who gave him valuable protection during his controversial career. Scipio Africanus was the leader of an intellectual circle including Gaius Laelius, and Terence soon gained admittance to it after arriving in Rome from Carthage.

reputation; and notwithstanding his extraordinary merit, it may be their countenance was not more than necessary.

The purity of his style, the delicacy of his turns, and the justness of his characters, were all of them beauties which the greater part of his audience were incapable of tasting; some of the coarsest strokes of Plautus, so severely censured by Horace, were more likely to affect the multitude—such who come with expectation to laugh out the last act of a play, and are better entertained with two or three unseasonable jests than with the artful solution of the *fable*.

As Terence excelled in his performances, so had he great advantages to encourage his undertakings, for he built most on the foundations of Menander; his plots were generally modelled, and his characters ready drawn to his hand. He copied Menander; and Menander had no less light in the formation of his characters from the observations of Theophrastus, of whom he was a disciple; and Theophrastus, it is known, was not only the disciple, but the immediate successor of Aristotle, the first and greatest judge of poetry. These were great models to design by; and the further advantage which Terence possessed towards giving his plays the due ornaments of purity of style, and justness of manners, was not less considerable: from the freedom of conversation, which was permitted him with Laelius and Scipio, two of the greatest and most polite men of his age. And indeed, the privilege of such a conversation is the only certain means of attaining to the perfection of dialogue.

If it has happened in any part of this comedy that I have gained a turn of style or expression more correct, or at least more corrigible than in those which I have formerly written, I must with equal pride and gratitude ascribe it to the honour of your Lordship's admitting me into your conversation, and that of a society where everybody else was so well worthy of you, in your retirement last summer from the town; for it was immediately after that this comedy was written. If I have failed in my performance it is only to be regretted, where there were so many not inferior either to a Scipio or a Laelius, that there

56 *laugh out* Q1, some copies of Q2 (laugh at Q2, Ww)

58 *fable* plot

61 *Menander*. Dramatist, writer of Greek New Comedy, drawn on by Terence in composing his own plays.

65 *Theophrastus*. Greek author of non-dramatic 'characters' and the model for English seventeenth-century writers of 'characters', such as Earle and Overbury.

should be one wanting, equal to the capacity of a Terence. 85

If I am not mistaken, poetry is almost the only art which has not yet laid claim to your Lordship's patronage. Architecture, and painting, to the great honour of our country, have flourished under your influence and protection. In the mean time poetry, the eldest sister of all arts and parent of most, seems to 90 have resigned her birthright by having neglected to pay her duty to your Lordship, and by permitting others of a later extraction to prepossess that place in your esteem to which none can pretend a better title. Poetry, in its nature, is sacred to the good and great; the relation between them is reciprocal, and 95 they are ever propitious to it. It is the privilege of poetry to address to them, and it is their prerogative alone to give it protection.

This received maxim is a general apology for all writers who consecrate their labours to great men; but I could wish at this 100 time that this address were exempted from the common pretense of all dedications; and that as I can distinguish your Lordship even among the most deserving, so this offering might become remarkable by some particular instance of respect which should assure your Lordship that I am, with all due sense 105 of your extreme worthiness and humanity.

MY LORD,
Your Lordship's
Most Obedient
and Most Humble 110
Servant,
WILL. CONGREVE

85 *to the capacity of* Q1, Q2 (in capacity to Ww)

87 *Architecture.* Montague built two great houses, Boughton House in Northamptonshire after the model of Versailles and Montagu House, Bloomsbury, also in the French style.

PROLOGUE

Spoken by Mr. Betterton

Of those few fools, who with ill stars are cursed,
Sure scribbling fools, called poets, fare the worst;
For they're a sort of fools which Fortune makes
And after she has made 'em fools, forsakes.
With Nature's oafs 'tis quite a different case, 5
For Fortune favours all her idiot race;
In her own nest the cuckoo eggs we find,
O'er which she broods to hatch the changeling kind.
No portion for her own she has to spare,
So much she dotes on her adopted care. 10
  Poets are bubbles, by the town drawn in,
Suffered at first some trifling stakes to win:
But what unequal hazards do they run!
Each time they write they venture all they've won;
The squire that's buttered still is sure to be undone. 15
This author heretofore has found your favour,
But pleads no merit from his past behaviour.
To build on that might prove a vain presumption
Should grants, to poets made, admit resumption;
And in Parnassus he must lose his seat 20
If that be found a forfeited estate.
  He owns, with toil he wrought the following scenes,
But if they're naught ne'er spare him for his pains,
Damn him the more; have no commiseration
For dullness on mature deliberation. 25
He swears he'll not resent one hissed-off scene
Nor, like those peevish wits, his play maintain,
Who, to assert their sense, your taste arraign.
Some plot we think he has, and some new thought;
Some humour too, no farce—but that's a fault. 30
Satire, he thinks, you ought not to expect:
For so reformed a town, who dares correct?
To please this time has been his sole pretence;

11 *bubbles* victims of fraud
15 *buttered* lavishly flattered
32 *so reformed a town* alluding to the Puritan attack, Collier's *A Short View of the Profaneness and Immorality of the English Stage* (1698)

He'll not instruct less it should give offence.
Should he by chance a knave or fool expose, 35
That hurts none here: sure here are none of those.
In short our play shall (with your leave to show it)
Give you one instance of a passive poet
Who to your judgements yields all resignation;
So save or damn, after your own discretion. 40

DRAMATIS PERSONAE

Men

FAINALL, *in love with Mrs. Marwood*	*Mr. Betterton*
MIRABELL, *in love with Mrs. Millamant*	*Mr. Verbruggen*
WITWOUD, PETULANT, } *followers of Mrs. Millamant*	*Mr. Bowen*, *Mr. Bowman*
SIR WILFULL WITWOUD, *half-brother to Witwoud, and nephew to Lady Wishfort*	*Mr. Underhill*
WAITWELL, *servant to Mirabell*	*Mr. Bright*

Women

LADY WISHFORT, *enemy to Mirabell for having falsely pretended love to her*	*Mrs. Leigh*
MRS MILLAMANT, *a fine lady, niece to Lady Wishfort, and loves Mirabell*	*Mrs. Bracegirdle*
MRS. MARWOOD, *friend to Mr. Fainall, and likes Mirabell*	*Mrs. Barry*
MRS. FAINALL, *daughter to Lady Wishfort and wife to Fainall, formerly friend to Mirabell*	*Mrs. Bowman*
FOIBLE, *woman to Lady Wishfort*	*Mrs. Willis*
MINCING, *woman to Mrs. Millamant*	*Mrs. Prince*

DANCERS, FOOTMEN, AND ATTENDANTS

SCENE LONDON

The time equal to that of the presentation

FAINALL The names identify character types; Fainall 'feigns all'.
MIRABELL 'admirable', and also perhaps 'an admirer of female beauty'
WITWOUD Compare Jonson's character *Sir Politic Would-be* for this kind of name.
MILLAMANT i.e. she has a thousand lovers; see II, 360–3

THE WAY OF THE WORLD
A Comedy

Act I, Scene i

A Chocolate-house

MIRABELL *and* FAINALL, [*rising from cards*]. BETTY *waiting*

MIRABELL
You are a fortunate man, Mr. Fainall.

FAINALL
Have we done?

MIRABELL
What you please. I'll play on to entertain you.

FAINALL
No, I'll give you your revenge another time, when you are not so indifferent; you are thinking of something else now, and play too negligently; the coldness of a losing gamester lessens the pleasure of the winner. I'd no more play with a man that slighted his ill fortune than I'd make love to a woman who undervalued the loss of her reputation.

MIRABELL
You have a taste extremely delicate, and are for refining on your pleasures.

FAINALL
Prithee, why so reserved? Something has put you out of humour.

MIRABELL
Not at all; I happen to be grave today, and you are gay: that's all.

FAINALL
Confess, Millamant and you quarrelled last night after I left you. My fair cousin has some humours that would tempt the patience of a Stoic. What, some coxcomb came in, and was well received by her, while you were by.

MIRABELL
Witwoud and Petulant; and what was worse, her aunt, your wife's mother, my evil genius; or to sum up all in her own name, my old Lady Wishfort came in.

17 *humours* moods

FAINALL

Oh there it is then! She has a lasting passion for you, and with reason. What, then my wife was there?

MIRABELL

Yes, and Mrs. Marwood and three or four more, whom I never saw before. Seeing me, they all put on their grave faces, whispered one another, then complained aloud of the vapours, and after fell into a profound silence.

FAINALL

They had a mind to be rid of you.

MIRABELL

For which reason I resolved not to stir. At last the good old lady broke through her painful taciturnity, with an invective against long visits. I would not have understood her, but Millamant joining in the argument, I rose and with a constrained smile told her, I thought nothing was so easy as to know when a visit began to be troublesome. She reddened and I withdrew, without expecting her reply.

FAINALL

You were to blame to resent what she spoke only in compliance with her aunt.

MIRABELL

She is more mistress of herself than to be under the necessity of such a resignation.

FAINALL

What? Though half her fortune depends upon her marrying with my lady's approbation?

MIRABELL

I was then in such a humour that I should have been better pleased if she had been less discreet.

FAINALL

Now I remember, I wonder not they were weary of you; last night was one of their cabal-nights. They have 'em three

28 *vapours* supposed exhalations from the organs of the body causing depression or nervous disorders

41 *fortune*. Millamant's fortune of £12,000 is rather larger than might have been likely for a lady in her social position in 1700, according to John Loftis, *Comedy and Society from Congreve to Fielding* (Stanford, 1959), pp. 46–8. This shows that traditional romantic spirit informs Congreve's design.

46 *cabal-nights*. The term is humorously exaggerated; serious political intrigue does not occupy the ladies. There is a reminiscence of *The Silent Woman*, I, i, where Truewit and Dauphine mockingly discuss the 'collegiate ladies'.

times a week, and meet by turns at one another's apartments, where they come together like the coroner's inquest, to sit upon the murdered reputations of the week. You and I are excluded, and it was once proposed that all the male sex should be excepted; but somebody moved that, to avoid scandal, there might be one man of the community; upon which motion Witwoud and Petulant were enrolled members.

MIRABELL

And who may have been the foundress of this sect? My Lady Wishfort, I warrant, who publishes her detestation of mankind; and full of the vigour of fifty-five, declares for a friend and ratafia, and let posterity shift for itself, she'll breed no more.

FAINALL

The discovery of your sham addresses to her, to conceal your love to her niece, has provoked this separation. Had you dissembled better, things might have continued in the state of nature.

MIRABELL

I did as much as man could, with any reasonable conscience. I proceeded to the very last act of flattery with her, and was guilty of a song in her commendation; nay, I got a friend to put her into a lampoon, and compliment her with the imputation of an affair with a young fellow, which I carried so far that I told her the malicious town took notice that she was grown fat of a sudden; and when she lay in of a dropsy, persuaded her she was reported to be in labour. The devil's in't, if an old woman is to be flattered further, unless a man should endeavour downright personally to debauch her: and that my virtue forbade me. But for the discovery of this amour, I am indebted to your friend, or your wife's friend, Mrs. Marwood.

FAINALL

What should provoke her to be your enemy, without she has made you advances which you have slighted? Women do not easily forgive omissions of that nature.

MIRABELL

She was always civil to me, till of late. I confess I am not one of those coxcombs who are apt to interpret a woman's good

73–4 *this amour* ed. (that amour Q1)
76 *without she* Q1, Q2 (unless she Ww)

57 *ratafia* cherry brandy made with peach stones and apricot stones
57 *shift* take care

manners to her prejudice, and think that she who does not refuse 'em everything, can refuse 'em nothing.

FAINALL

You are a gallant man, Mirabell; and though you may have cruelty enough not to satisfy a lady's longing, you have too much generosity not to be tender of her honour. Yet you speak with an indifference which seems to be affected, and confesses you are conscious of a negligence.

MIRABELL

You pursue the argument with a distrust that seems to be unaffected, and confesses you are conscious of a concern, for which the lady is more indebted to you than your wife.

FAINALL

Fie, fie, friend! If you grow censorious I must leave you. I'll look upon the gamesters in the next room.

MIRABELL

Who are they?

FAINALL

Petulant and Witwoud. [*to* BETTY] Bring me some chocolate. *Exit*

MIRABELL

Betty, what says your clock?

BETTY

Turned of the last canonical hour sir. *Exit*

MIRABELL

How pertinently the jade answers me! Ha? Almost one o'clock! (*looking on his watch*) Oh, y'are come!

Enter a SERVANT

Well, is the grand affair over? You have been something tedious.

SERVANT

Sir, there's such coupling at Pancras that they stand behind one another as 'twere in a country dance. Ours was the last couple to lead up; and no hopes appearing of dispatch, besides, the parson growing hoarse, we were afraid his lungs would have failed before it came to our turn; so we drove

90 *than your wife* Q1, Q2 (than is your wife Ww)

96 *canonical hour.* 8 a.m. to noon were the hours during which legal marriages in church could take place.

101 *Pancras.* Summers cites *The Modish Wife* (1676) V, iii: 'What think you of taking a Coach to *Pancras*-Church . . . for that is a place of Priviledge and Liberty to Marry without Licences, and at any time'.

round to Duke's Place and there they were riveted in a trice.

MIRABELL

So, so, you are sure they are married.

SERVANT

Married and bedded sir: I am witness.

MIRABELL

Have you the certificate?

SERVANT

Here it is sir.

MIRABELL

Has the tailor brought Waitwell's clothes home, and the new liveries?

SERVANT

Yes sir.

MIRABELL

That's well. Do you go home again, d'ye hear, and adjourn the consummation till farther order. Bid Waitwell shake his ears, and Dame Partlet rustle up her feathers, and meet me at one o'clock by Rosamond's Pond, that I may see her before she returns to her lady; and as you tender your ears, be secret. *Exit* SERVANT

Enter FAINALL [*and* BETTY]

FAINALL

Joy of your success, Mirabell; you look pleased.

MIRABELL

Ay, I have been engaged in a matter of some sort of mirth which is not yet ripe for discovery. I am glad this is not a cabal-night. I wonder, Fainall, that you who are married, and of consequence should be discreet, will suffer your wife to be of such a party.

FAINALL

Faith, I am not jealous. Besides, most who are engaged are women and relations; and for the men, they are of a kind too contemptible to give scandal.

115 *d'ye* ed. (d'ee Q1) this emendation followed through the text

106 *Duke's Place* in Aldgate, now Duke Street. St James's Church there was notorious for irregular marriages, vulgarly called Fleet weddings (Summers).

117 *Dame Partlet* wife of Chanticleer in the fable; see Chaucer, *The Nun's Priest's Tale.*

118 *Rosamond's Pond* a favourite meeting-place in St James's Park around which Charles II planted groves (Lynch)

MIRABELL

I am of another opinion. The greater the coxcomb, always the more the scandal; for a woman who is not a fool can have but one reason for associating with a man that is.

FAINALL

Are you jealous as often as you see Witwoud entertained by Millamant?

MIRABELL

Of her understanding I am, if not of her person.

FAINALL

You do her wrong; for to give her her due, she has wit.

MIRABELL

She has beauty enough to make any man think so, and complaisance enough not to contradict him who shall tell her so.

FAINALL

For a passionate lover, methinks you are a man somewhat too discerning in the failings of your mistress.

MIRABELL

And for a discerning man, somewhat too passionate a lover; for I like her with all her faults, nay, like her for her faults. Her follies are so natural, or so artful, that they become her; and those affectations which in another woman would be odious, serve but to make her more agreeable. I'll tell thee Fainall, she once used me with that insolence, that in revenge I took her to pieces, sifted her, and separated her failings; I studied 'em, and got 'em by rote. The catalogue was so large, that I was not without hopes, one day or other to hate her heartily; to which end I so used myself to think of 'em, that at length, contrary to my design and expectation, they gave me every hour less and less disturbance, till in a few days it became habitual to me to remember 'em without being displeased. They are now grown as familiar to me as my own frailties; and in all probability in a little time longer I shall like 'em as well.

FAINALL

Marry her, marry her! Be half as well acquainted with her charms as you are with her defects, and my life on't, you are your own man again.

MIRABELL

Say you so?

132 *man that is* Q1, Q2 (man who is one Ww)

---

135 *understanding* intellect; capacity to comprehend and judge

159 *your own man* heart-free, not in love

FAINALL
Ay, ay, I have experience: I have a wife, and so forth.

Enter MESSENGER

MESSENGER
Is one Squire Witwoud here?

BETTY
Yes; what's your business?

MESSENGER
I have a letter for him from his brother Sir Wilfull, which I am charged to deliver into his own hands.

BETTY
He's in the next room, friend – that way. *Exit* MESSENGER

MIRABELL
What, is the chief of that noble family in town, Sir Wilfull Witwoud?

FAINALL
He is expected today. Do you know him?

MIRABELL
I have seen him, he promises to be an extraordinary person. I think you have the honour to be related to him.

FAINALL
Yes; he is half-brother to this Witwoud by a former wife, who was sister to my Lady Wishfort, my wife's mother. If you marry Millamant you must call cousins too.

MIRABELL
I had rather be his relation than his acquaintance.

FAINALL
He comes to town in order to equip himself for travel.

MIRABELL
For travel! Why, the man that I mean is above forty!

FAINALL
No matter for that; 'tis for the honour of England that all Europe should know we have blockheads of all ages.

MIRABELL
I wonder there is not an act of parliament to save the credit of the nation and prohibit the exportation of fools.

FAINALL
By no means, 'tis better as 'tis. 'Tis better to trade with a little loss, than to be quite eaten up with being overstocked.

MIRABELL
Pray, are the follies of this knight-errant and those of the squire his brother anything related?

FAINALL

Not at all; Witwoud grows by the knight like a medlar grafted on a crab; one will melt in your mouth, and t'other set your teeth on edge; one is all pulp and the other all core.

MIRABELL

So one will be rotten before he be ripe, and the other will be rotten without ever being ripe at all.

FAINALL

Sir Wilfull is an odd mixture of bashfulness and obstinacy; but when he's drunk he's as loving as the monster in *The Tempest*, and much after the same manner. To give t'other his due, he has something of good nature, and does not always want wit.

MIRABELL

Not always; but as often as his memory fails him, and his commonplace of comparisons. He is a fool with a good memory and some few scraps of other folks' wit. He is one whose conversation can never be approved, yet it is now and then to be endured. He has indeed one good quality, he is not exceptious; for he so passionately affects the reputation of understanding raillery, that he will construe an affront into a jest, and call downright rudeness and ill language satire and fire.

FAINALL

If you have a mind to finish his picture, you have an opportunity to do it at full length. Behold the original.

Enter WITWOUD

WITWOUD

Afford me your compassion, my dears; pity me Fainall, Mirabell, pity me!

MIRABELL

I do, from my soul.

194 *t'other* ed. (the t'other Q1, Q2)

---

186 *medlar* a sort of apple, eaten when decayed to a soft pulpy state; see *As You Like It*, III, ii, 108–10: 'for you'll be rotten ere you be half ripe, and that's the right virtue of the medlar.'

187 *crab* a sour wild apple, proverbial for its tartness

193–4 *monster in The Tempest* Purcell composed new music in 1690 for the highly popular Dryden-Davenant opera based on Shakespeare's play

198 *commonplace* a commonplace book, in which memorable sayings and verses were recorded.

202 *exceptious* disposed to make objections

FAINALL
Why, what's the matter?
WITWOUD
No letters for me, Betty?
BETTY
Did not the messenger bring you one but now, sir?
WITWOUD
Ay, but no other?
BETTY
No sir.
WITWOUD
That's hard, that's very hard. A messenger, a mule, a beast of burden, he has brought me a letter from the fool my brother, as heavy as a panegyric in a funeral sermon, or a copy of commendatory verses from one poet to another. And what's worse, 'tis as sure a forerunner of the author as an epistle dedicatory.
MIRABELL
A fool, and your brother, Witwoud!
WITWOUD
Ay, ay, my half-brother. My half-brother he is, no nearer, upon honour.
MIRABELL
Then 'tis possible he may be but half a fool.
WITWOUD
Good, good, Mirabell *le drôle*! Good, good, hang him, don't let's talk of him. Fainall, how does your lady? Gad, I say anything in the world to get this fellow out of my head. I beg pardon that I should ask a man of pleasure, and the town, a question at once so foreign and domestic. But I talk like an old maid at a marriage, I don't know what I say; but she's the best woman in the world.
FAINALL
'Tis well you don't know what you say, or else your commendation would go near to make me either vain or jealous.
WITWOUD
No man in town lives well with a wife but Fainall: your judgement Mirabell?
MIRABELL
You had better step and ask his wife if you would be credibly informed.

213 *the messenger* Q1, Q2 (a messenger Ww)
231 *but she's* Q1, Q2, W1 (she's W2)

WITWOUD
Mirabell.
MIRABELL
Ay. 240
WITWOUD
My dear, I ask ten thousand pardons – Gad, I have forgot what I was going to say to you.
MIRABELL
I thank you heartily, heartily.
WITWOUD
No, but prithee excuse me, my memory is such a memory.
MIRABELL
Have a care of such apologies, Witwoud; for I never knew a 245 fool but he affected to complain either of the spleen or his memory.
FAINALL
What have you done with Petulant?
WITWOUD
He's reckoning his money – my money it was. I have no luck today. 250
FAINALL
You may allow him to win of you at play, for you are sure to be too hard for him at repartee. Since you monopolise the wit that is between you, the fortune must be his of course.
MIRABELL
I don't find that Petulant confesses the superiority of wit to be your talent, Witwoud. 255
WITWOUD
Come, come, you are malicious now, and would breed debates. Petulant's my friend, and a very honest fellow, and a very pretty fellow, and has a smattering – faith and troth a pretty deal – of an odd sort of a small wit. Nay, I'll do him justice. I'm his friend, I won't wrong him neither. 260 And if he had but any judgement in the world he would not be altogether contemptible. Come, come, don't detract from the merits of my friend.
FAINALL
You don't take your friend to be over-nicely bred.
WITWOUD
No no, hang him, the rogue has no manners at all, that I must 265

257–8 *honest fellow, and a very pretty* Q1, Q2, W1 (pretty fellow, and a very honest W2)
260 *him neither* Q1, Q2 (him Ww)
261 *had but any* Q1, Q2 (had any Ww)

own; no more breeding than a bum-baily, that I grant you. 'Tis pity, faith; the fellow has fire and life.

MIRABELL

What, courage?

WITWOUD

Hum, faith, I don't know as to that – I can't say as to that. Yes, faith, in a controversy he'll contradict anybody. 270

MIRABELL

Though'twere a man whom he feared or a woman whom he loved.

WITWOUD

Well, well, he does not always think before he speaks; we have all our failings. You are too hard upon him, you are faith. Let me excuse him. I can defend most of his faults, except 275 one or two. One he has, that's the truth on't, if he were my brother I could not acquit him – that indeed I could wish were otherwise.

MIRABELL

Ay, marry, what's that, Witwoud?

WITWOUD

Oh pardon me; expose the infirmities of my friend? No, my 280 dear, excuse me there.

FAINALL

What, I warrant he's insincere, or 'tis some such trifle.

WITWOUD

No, no, what if he be? 'Tis no matter for that; his wit will excuse that. A wit should no more be sincere, than a woman constant. One argues a decay of parts as t'other of beauty. 285

MIRABELL

Maybe you think him too positive?

WITWOUD

No, no, his being positive is an incentive to argument, and keeps up conversation.

FAINALL

Too illiterate.

WITWOUD

That! That's his happiness. His want of learning gives him 290 the more opportunities to show his natural parts.

267 *pity, faith* Q1, Q2 (pity Ww)
282 *insincere* ed. (unsincere Q1, Q2, Ww)

---

266 *bum-baily* 'a bailiff of the meanest kind; one employed in arrests' (Dr Johnson's Dictionary)

MIRABELL
He wants words.
WITWOUD
Ay; but I like him for that now; for his want of words gives me the pleasure very often to explain his meaning.
FAINALL
He's impudent. 295
WITWOUD
No; that's not it.
MIRABELL
Vain.
WITWOUD
No.
MIRABELL
What, he speaks unseasonable truths sometimes, because he has not wit enough to invent an evasion. 300
WITWOUD
Truths! Ha, ha, ha! No, no, since you will have it, I mean he never speaks truth at all – that's all. He will lie like a chambermaid, or a woman of quality's porter. Now that is a fault.

Enter COACHMAN

COACHMAN
Is Master Petulant here, mistress? 305
BETTY
Yes.
COACHMAN
Three gentlewomen in the coach would speak with him.
FAINALL
Oh brave Petulant, three!
BETTY
I'll tell him.
COACHMAN
You must bring two dishes of chocolate and a glass of cinnamon-water. 310

Exit

WITWOUD
That should be for two fasting strumpets, and a bawd troubled with wind. Now you may know what the three are.

307 *the coach* Q1, Q2 (a coach Ww)

310–11 *cinnamon-water* a digestive cordial flavoured with cinnamon

MIRABELL
You are very free with your friend's acquaintance.

WITWOUD
Ay, ay, friendship without freedom is as dull as love without enjoyment, or wine without toasting; but to tell you a secret, these are trulls that he allows coach-hire, and something more, by the week, to call on him once a day at public places.

MIRABELL
How!

WITWOUD
You shall see he won't go to 'em because there's no more company here to take notice of him. Why this is nothing to what he used to do; before he found out this way, I have known him call for himself.

FAINALL
Call for himself? What dost thou mean?

WITWOUD
Mean? Why, he would slip you out of this chocolate-house, just when you had been talking to him. As soon as your back was turned, whip! He was gone. Then trip to his lodging, clap on a hood and scarf, and mask, slap into a hackney-coach, and drive hither to the door again in a trice; where he would send in for himself, that I mean, call for himself, wait for himself, nay and what's more, not finding himself, sometimes leave a letter for himself.

MIRABELL
I confess this is something extraordinary. I believe he waits for himself now, he is so long a-coming; Oh, I ask his pardon.

Enter PETULANT

BETTY
Sir, the coach stays.

PETULANT
Well, well, I come. 'Sbud, a man had as good be a professed midwife as a professed whoremaster at this rate. To be knocked up, and raised, at all hours, and in all places! Pox on 'em! I won't come. D'ye hear, tell 'em I won't come. Let 'em snivel and cry their hearts out.

FAINALL
You are very cruel, Petulant.

PETULANT
All's one, let it pass. I have a humour to be cruel.

317 *trulls that* Q1, Q2 (trulls whom Ww)

MIRABELL

I hope they are not persons of condition that you use at this rate.

PETULANT

Condition? Condition's a dried fig, if I am not in humour. By this hand, if they were your—a—a—your what-d'ye-call-'ems themselves, they must wait or rub off, if I want appetite.

MIRABELL

What-d'ye-call-'ems! What are they, Witwoud?

WITWOUD

Empresses, my dear—by your what-d'ye-call-'ems he means sultana queens.

PETULANT

Ay, Roxolanas.

MIRABELL

Cry you mercy.

FAINALL

Witwoud says they are—

PETULANT

What does he say th'are?

WITWOUD

I? Fine ladies I say.

PETULANT

Pass on, Witwoud. Harkee, by this light, his relations: two co-heiresses his cousins, and an old aunt, that loves cater-wauling better than a conventicle.

WITWOUD

Ha, ha, ha! I had a mind to see how the rogue would come off—ha, ha, ha. Gad I can't be angry with him, if he said they were my mother and my sisters.

MIRABELL

No!

WITWOUD

No; the rogue's wit and readiness of invention charm me; dear Petulant.

358 *that loves* Q1, Q2 (who loves Ww)

---

344 *condition* gentle birth

352 *Roxolanas.* Roxolana is the wife of Sultan Solyman the Magnificent in Davenant's *The Siege of Rhodes.*

359 *conventicle.* A meeting of Nonconformists, religious Dissenters: the opprobrium attaching to the term was a consequence of the outlawing of such meetings at the Restoration, though by 1700 they were no longer illegal. Puritan sects were notorious for their singing (at least among non-Puritans).

BETTY
They are gone sir, in great anger.

PETULANT
Enough, let 'em trundle. Anger helps complexion, saves paint.

FAINALL
This continence is all dissembled; this is in order to have something to brag of the next time he makes court to Millamant, and swear he has abandoned the whole sex for her sake.

MIRABELL
Have you not left off your impudent pretensions there yet? I shall cut your throat sometime or other, Petulant, about that business.

PETULANT
Ay, ay, let that pass; there are other throats to be cut—

MIRABELL
Meaning mine, sir?

PETULANT
Not I—I mean nobody—I know nothing—but there are uncles and nephews in the world—and they may be rivals—what then? All's one for that—

MIRABELL
How! Harkee, Petulant, come hither. Explain, or I shall call your interpreter.

PETULANT
Explain? I know nothing. Why, you have an uncle, have you not, lately come to town, and lodges by my Lady Wishfort's?

MIRABELL
True.

PETULANT
Why, that's enough. You and he are not friends; and if he should marry and have a child, you may be disinherited, ha?

MIRABELL
Where hast thou stumbled upon all this truth?

PETULANT
All's one for that. Why then, say I know something.

367 *trundle* slang: 'make off'

376 *let that pass* . . . cf. *Henry V*, II, i, 20–25: 'I cannot tell; things must be as they may. Men may sleep, and they may have their throats about them at that time; and some say knives have edges. It must be as it may; though patience be a tired mare, yet she will plod. There must be conclusions. Well, I cannot tell.'

MIRABELL

Come, thou art an honest fellow, Petulant, and shalt make love to my mistress, thou shalt i'faith. What hast thou heard of my uncle? 390

PETULANT

I? Nothing, I. If throats are to be cut, let swords clash; snug's the word; I shrug and am silent.

MIRABELL

Oh raillery, raillery. Come, I know thou art in the women's secrets. What, you're a cabalist. I know you stayed at Millamant's last night, after I went. Was there any mention made of my uncle, or me? Tell me. If thou hadst but good nature equal to thy wit, Petulant, Tony Witwoud, who is now thy competitor in fame, would show as dim by thee as a dead whiting's eye by a pearl of orient. He would no more be seen by thee, than Mercury is by the sun. Come, I'm sure thou wilt tell me. 395 400

PETULANT

If I do, will you grant me commonsense then for the future.

MIRABELL

Faith I'll do what I can for thee; and I'll pray that heaven may grant it thee in the meantime. 405

PETULANT

Well, harkee.

FAINALL

Petulant and you both will find Mirabell as warm a rival as a lover.

WITWOUD

Pshaw, pshaw! That she laughs at Petulant is plain; and for my part—but that it is almost a fashion to admire her, I should—harkee—to tell you a secret, but let it go no further—between friends, I shall never break my heart for her. 410

FAINALL

How!

WITWOUD

She's handsome; but she's a sort of an uncertain woman. 415

403 *wilt* ed. (wo't Q1, Q2, Ww)

---

401 *whiting's eye.* The whiting has pearly white flesh; its dead eye would be dull and glazed; and there may be a play upon the proverbial meaning of whiting's eye = amorous leer.

401 *pearl of orient* brilliant and precious pearls, as distinct from those found in European waters, which are dull

FAINALL
I thought you had died for her.
WITWOUD
Umh—no—
FAINALL
She has wit.
WITWOUD
'Tis what she will hardly allow anybody else. Now, demme, I should hate that, if she were as handsome as Cleopatra. Mirabell is not so sure of her as he thinks for.
FAINALL
Why do you think so?
WITWOUD
We stayed pretty late there last night, and heard something of an uncle to Mirabell who is lately come to town, and is between him and the best part of his estate. Mirabell and he are at some distance, as my Lady Wishfort has been told; and you know she hates Mirabell worse than a quaker hates a parrot, or than a fishmonger hates a hard frost. Whether this uncle has seen Mrs. Millamant or not, I cannot say; but there were items of such a treaty being in embryo; and if it should come to life, poor Mirabell would be in some sort unfortunately fobbed, i'faith.
FAINALL
'Tis impossible Millamant should hearken to it.
WITWOUD
Faith, my dear, I can't tell; she's a woman and a kind of a humorist.
MIRABELL
And this is the sum of what you could collect last night.
PETULANT
The quintessence. Maybe Witwoud knows more, he stayed longer; besides, they never mind him; they say anything before him.
MIRABELL
I thought you had been the greatest favourite.

427–8 *worse than a quaker hates a parrot.* A quaker's pacific principles and plain dress and manners contrast with the gaudy plumage and chatter of a parrot.
428 *a fishmonger hates a hard frost* because ice makes fishing impossible
432 *fobbed*, tricked, cheated
435 *humorist* capricious person

PETULANT

Ay, *tête à tête*; but not in public, because I make remarks.

MIRABELL

Do you?

PETULANT

Ay, ay, pox, I'm malicious, man. Now he's soft you know, they are not in awe of him—the fellow's well-bred, he's what you call a—what-d'ye-call-'em—a fine gentleman; but he's silly withal.

MIRABELL

I thank you, I know as much as my curiosity requires. Fainall, are you for the Mall?

FAINALL

Ay, I'll take a turn before dinner.

WITWOUD

Ay, we'll all walk in the park; the ladies talked of being there.

MIRABELL

I thought you were obliged to watch for your brother Sir Wilfull's arrival.

WITWOUD

No, no, he comes to his aunt's, my Lady Wishfort; pox on him, I shall be troubled with him too; what shall I do with the fool?

PETULANT

Beg him for his estate, that I may beg you afterwards, and so have but one trouble with you both.

WITWOUD

Oh rare Petulant! Thou art as quick as a fire in a frosty morning; thou shalt to the Mall with us; and we'll be very severe.

PETULANT

Enough. I'm in a humour to be severe.

MIRABELL

Are you? Pray then walk by yourselves—let not us be accessory to your putting the ladies out of countenance with your senseless ribaldry, which you roar out aloud as often as

441 *tête à tête* ed. (teste a teste Q1, Q2)
442 *Do you?* Q1, Q2 (You do? Ww)
459 *a fire* Q1, Q2 (fire Ww)

---

448 *the Mall.* A gravel walk bordered by trees in St James's Park, originally the alley in which the game of mall was played, later a fashionable promenade. Etherege sets II, iii, of *The Man of Mode* in the Mall.

they pass by you; and when you have made a handsome woman blush, then you think you have been severe.

PETULANT

What, what? Then let 'em either show their innocence by not understanding what they hear, or else show their discretion by not hearing what they would not be thought to understand.

MIRABELL

But hast not thou then sense enough to know that thou ought'st to be most ashamed thyself, when thou hast put another out of countenance?

PETULANT

Not I, by this hand; I always take blushing either for a sign of guilt, or ill-breeding.

MIRABELL

I confess you ought to think so. You are in the right, that you may plead the error of your judgement in defence of your practice.

Where modesty's ill manners, 'tis but fit
That impudence and malice pass for wit. *Exeunt*

Act II, Scene i

St. James's Park

Enter MRS. FAINALL *and* MRS. MARWOOD

MRS. FAINALL

Ay, ay, dear Marwood, if we will be happy, we must find the means in ourselves, and among ourselves. Men are ever in extremes, either doting or averse. While they are lovers, if they have fire and sense their jealousies are insupportable; and when they cease to love (we ought to think at least) they loathe. They look upon us with horror and distaste; they meet us like the ghosts of what we were, and as such fly from us.

MRS. MARWOOD

True, 'tis an unhappy circumstance of life, that love should ever die before us, and that the man so often should outlive the lover. But say what you will, 'tis better to be left than never to have been loved. To pass our youth in dull indifference, to refuse the sweets of life because they once must leave us, is as preposterous as to wish to have been born old, because we one day must be old. For my part, my youth may wear and waste, but it shall never rust in my possession.

7 *as such* Q1, Q2 (as from such Ww)

MRS. FAINALL

Then it seems you dissemble an aversion to mankind only in compliance with my mother's humour.

MRS. MARWOOD

Certainly—to be free. I have no taste of those insipid dry discourses with which our sex, of force, must entertain themselves apart from men. We may affect endearments to each other, profess eternal friendships, and seem to dote like lovers; but 'tis not in our natures long to persevere. Love will resume his empire in our breasts, and every heart, or soon, or late, receive and readmit him as its lawful tyrant.

MRS. FAINALL

Bless me, how have I been deceived! Why, you profess a libertine!

MRS. MARWOOD

You see my friendship by my freedom. Come, be as sincere; acknowledge that your sentiments agree with mine.

MRS. FAINALL

Never.

MRS. MARWOOD

You hate mankind.

MRS. FAINALL

Heartily, inveterately.

MRS. MARWOOD

Your husband.

MRS. FAINALL

Most transcendently! Ay, though I say it, meritoriously.

MRS. MARWOOD

Give me your hand upon it.

MRS. FAINALL

There.

MRS. MARWOOD

I join with you; what I have said has been to try you.

MRS. FAINALL

Is it possible? Dost thou hate those vipers, men?

MRS. MARWOOD

I have done hating 'em, and am now come to despise 'em; the next thing I have to do, is eternally to forget 'em.

MRS. FAINALL

There spoke the spirit of an Amazon, a Penthesilea.

17 *compliance with* Q1, Q2 (compliance to Ww)

---

19 *of force* of necessity

40 *Penthesilea* Amazonian queen

MRS. MARWOOD

And yet I am thinking, sometimes, to carry my aversion further.

MRS. FAINALL

How?

MRS. MARWOOD

Faith, by marrying; if I could but find one that loved me very well, and would be thoroughly sensible of ill usage, I think I should do myself the violence of undergoing the ceremony.

MRS. FAINALL

You would not make him a cuckold?

MRS. MARWOOD

No; but I'd make him believe I did, and that's as bad.

MRS. FAINALL

Why, had not you as good do it?

MRS. MARWOOD

Oh if he should ever discover it, he would then know the worst, and be out of his pain; but I would have him ever to continue upon the rack of fear and jealousy.

MRS. FAINALL

Ingenious mischief! Would thou wert married to Mirabell.

MRS. MARWOOD

Would I were.

MRS. FAINALL

You change colour.

MRS. MARWOOD

Because I hate him.

MRS. FAINALL

So do I; but I can hear him named. But what reason have you to hate him in particular?

MRS. MARWOOD

I never loved him; he is, and always was insufferably proud.

MRS. FAINALL

By the reason you give for your aversion, one would think it dissembled; for you have laid a fault to his charge of which his enemies must acquit him.

MRS. MARWOOD

Oh, then it seems you are one of his favourable enemies. Methinks you look a little pale—and now you flush again.

MRS. FAINALL

Do I? I think I am a little sick o' the sudden.

MRS. MARWOOD

What ails you?

MRS. FAINALL
My husband; don't you see him? He turned short upon me unawares and has almost overcome me.

Enter FAINALL *and* MIRABELL

MRS. MARWOOD
Ha, ha, ha! He comes opportunely for you.
MRS. FAINALL
For you, for he has brought Mirabell with him.
FAINALL
My dear.
MRS. FAINALL
My soul.
FAINALL
You don't look well today, child.
MRS. FAINALL
D'ye think so?
MIRABELL
He is the only man that does, madam.
MRS. FAINALL
The only man that would tell me so, at least; and the only man from whom I could hear it without mortification.
FAINALL
Oh, my dear, I am satisfied of your tenderness; I know you cannot resent anything from me, especially what is an effect of my concern.
MRS. FAINALL
Mr. Mirabell, my mother interrupted you in a pleasant relation last night; I would fain hear it out.
MIRABELL
The persons concerned in that affair have yet a tolerable reputation; I am afraid Mr. Fainall will be censorious.
MRS. FAINALL
He has a humour more prevailing than his curiosity, and will willingly dispense with the hearing of one scandalous story, to avoid giving an occasion to make another by being seen to walk with his wife. This way Mr. Mirabell, and I dare promise you will oblige us both.

Exeunt MRS. FAINALL *and* MIRABELL

FAINALL
Excellent creature! Well sure if I should live to be rid of my wife, I should be a miserable man.
MRS. MARWOOD
Ay!

FAINALL

For having only that one hope, the accomplishment of it of consequence must put an end to all my hopes; and what a wretch is he who must survive his hopes! Nothing remains when that day comes, but to sit down and weep like Alexander, when he wanted other worlds to conquer.

MRS. MARWOOD

Will you not follow 'em?

FAINALL

Faith, I think not.

MRS. MARWOOD

Pray let us; I have a reason.

FAINALL

You are not jealous?

MRS. MARWOOD

Of whom?

FAINALL

Of Mirabell.

MRS. MARWOOD

If I am, is it inconsistent with my love to you that I am tender of your honour?

FAINALL

You would intimate then, as if there were a fellow-feeling between my wife and him.

MRS. MARWOOD

I think she does not hate him to that degree she would be thought.

FAINALL

But he, I fear, is too insensible.

MRS. MARWOOD

It may be you are deceived.

FAINALL

It may be so. I do not now begin to apprehend it.

MRS. MARWOOD

What?

FAINALL

That I have been deceived, madam, and you are false.

112 *I do not now* ed. (I do now Q1)

97 *Alexander* reminiscent of Molière, *Dom Juan*, when Juan declares his libertine philosophy: 'Il n'est rien qui puisse arrêter l'impétuosité de mes désirs: je me sens un coeur à aimer toute la terre; et comme Alexandre, je souhaiterais qu'il y eût d'autres mondes, pour y pouvoir étendre mes conquêtes amoureuses.' (I, ii).

MRS. MARWOOD

That I am false! What mean you?

FAINALL

To let you know I see through all your little arts. Come, you both love him; and both have equally dissembled your aversion. Your mutual jealousies of one another have made you clash till you have both struck fire. I have seen the warm confession reddening on your cheeks and sparkling from your eyes.

MRS. MARWOOD

You do me wrong.

FAINALL

I do not. 'Twas for my ease to oversee and wilfully neglect the gross advances made him by my wife; that by permitting her to be engaged, I might continue unsuspected in my pleasures, and take you oftener to my arms in full security. But could you think, because the nodding husband would not wake, that e'er the watchful lover slept?

MRS. MARWOOD

And wherewithal can you reproach me?

FAINALL

With infidelity, with loving of another, with love of Mirabell.

MRS. MARWOOD

'Tis false. I challenge you to show an instance that can confirm your groundless accusation. I hate him.

FAINALL

And wherefore do you hate him? He is insensible, and your resentment follows his neglect. An instance? The injuries you have done him are a proof: your interposing in his love. What cause had you to make discoveries of his pretended passion? To undeceive the credulous aunt, and be the officious obstacle of his match with Millamant.

MRS. MARWOOD

My obligations to my lady urged me. I had professed a friendship to her, and could not see her easy nature so abused by that dissembler.

FAINALL

What! Was it conscience then! Professed a friendship! Oh the pious friendships of the female sex!

MRS. MARWOOD

More tender, more sincere, and more enduring, than all the

130 *loving of another* Q1, Q2 (loving another Ww)

vain and empty vows of men, whether professing love to us, or mutual faith to one another. 145

FAINALL

Ha, ha, ha! You are my wife's friend too.

MRS. MARWOOD

Shame and ingratitude! Do you reproach me? You, you, upbraid me? Have I been false to her through strict fidelity to you, and sacrificed my friendship to keep my love inviolate, 150 and have you the baseness to charge me with the guilt, unmindful of the merit! To you it should be meritorious that I have been vicious: and do you reflect that guilt upon me, which should lie buried in your bosom?

FAINALL

You misinterpret my reproof. I meant but to remind you of 155 the slight account you once could make of strictest ties, when set in competition with your love to me.

MRS. MARWOOD

'Tis false, you urged it with deliberate malice—'twas spoke in scorn, and I never will forgive it.

FAINALL

Your guilt, not your resentment, begets your rage. If yet 160 you loved, you could forgive a jealousy; but you are stung to find you are discovered.

MRS. MARWOOD

It shall be all discovered—you too shall be discovered! Be sure you shall! I can but be exposed; if I do it myself I shall prevent your baseness. 165

FAINALL

Why, what will you do?

MRS. MARWOOD

Disclose it to your wife; own what has passed between us.

FAINALL

Frenzy!

MRS. MARWOOD

By all my wrongs, I'll do't! I'll publish to the world the injuries you have done me, both in my fame and fortune: 170 with both I trusted you, you—bankrupt in honour, as indigent of wealth!

FAINALL

Your fame I have preserved; your fortune has been bestowed as the prodigality of your love would have it, in pleasures

157 *competition* Q1-Ww (comparison *Lynch*)

165 *prevent* anticipate

which we both have shared. Yet had not you been false, I had ere this repaid it. 'Tis true! Had you permitted Mirabell with Millamant to have stolen their marriage, my lady had been incensed beyond all means of reconcilement. Millamant had forfeited the moiety of her fortune, which then would have descended to my wife; and wherefore did I marry, but to make lawful prize of a rich widow's wealth, and squander it on love and you?

MRS. MARWOOD

Deceit and frivolous pretence!

FAINALL

Death, am I not married? What's pretence? Am I not imprisoned, fettered? Have I not a wife? Nay, a wife that was a widow, a young widow, a handsome widow; and would be again a widow, but that I have a heart of proof and something of a constitution, to bustle through the ways of wedlock and this world. Will you yet be reconciled to truth and me?

MRS. MARWOOD

Impossible; truth and you are inconsistent! I hate you, and shall for ever.

FAINALL

For loving you?

MRS. MARWOOD

I loathe the name of love, after such usage; and next to the guilt with which you would asperse me, I scorn you most. Farewell.

FAINALL

Nay, we must not part thus.

MRS. MARWOOD

Let me go!

FAINALL

Come, I'm sorry.

MRS. MARWOOD

I care not—let me go—break my hands, do! I'd leave 'em to get loose.

FAINALL

I would not hurt you for the world. Have I no other hold to keep you here?

MRS. MARWOOD

Well, I have deserved it all.

179 *moiety* half

188 *bustle* possibly reminiscent of *Richard III*, I, i, 152

FAINALL
You know I love you. 205

MRS. MARWOOD
Poor dissembling—oh that—well, it is not yet—

FAINALL
What? What is it not? What is it not yet? It is not yet too late—

MRS. MARWOOD
No, it is not yet too late; I have that comfort.

FAINALL
It is, to love another. 210

MRS. MARWOOD
But not to loathe, detest, abhor mankind, myself, and the whole treacherous world.

FAINALL
Nay, this is extravagance! Come, I ask your pardon—no tears—I was to blame; I could not love you and be easy in my doubts. Pray forbear—I believe you. I'm convinced I've 215 done you wrong, and any way, every way, will make amends. I'll hate my wife yet more, damn her! I'll part with her, rob her of all she's worth, and we'll retire somewhere, anywhere, to another world—I'll marry thee—be pacified—'sdeath, they come! Hide your face, your tears! You have a mask, wear it a 220 moment. This way, this way, be persuaded! *Exeunt*

Enter MIRABELL *and* MRS. FAINALL

MRS. FAINALL
They are here yet.

MIRABELL
They are turning into the other walk.

MRS. FAINALL
While I only hated my husband, I could bear to see him; but since I have despised him, he's too offensive. 225

MIRABELL
Oh you should hate with prudence.

MRS. FAINALL
Yes, for I have loved with indiscretion.

MIRABELL
You should have just so much disgust for your husband as may be sufficient to make you relish your lover.

215–16 *I've done* Q1 (I have done Q2, Ww)
218 *we'll retire* ed. (will retire Q1, Q2)

MRS. FAINALL

You have been the cause that I have loved without bounds, and would you set limits to that aversion of which you have been the occasion? Why did you make me marry this man?

MIRABELL

Why do we daily commit disagreeable and dangerous actions? To save that idol, reputation. If the familiarities of our loves had produced that consequence, of which you were apprehensive, where could you have fixed a father's name with credit, but on a husband? I knew Fainall to be a man lavish of his morals: an interested and professing friend, a false and a designing lover; yet one whose wit and outward fair behaviour have gained a reputation with the town, enough to make that woman stand excused, who has suffered herself to be won by his address. A better man ought not to have been sacrificed to the occasion; a worse had not answered to the purpose. When you are weary of him, you know your remedy.

MRS. FAINALL

I ought to stand in some degree of credit with you, Mirabell.

MIRABELL

In justice to you, I have made you privy to my whole design, and put it in your power to ruin or advance my fortune.

MRS. FAINALL

Whom have you instructed to represent your pretended uncle?

MIRABELL

Waitwell, my servant.

MRS. FAINALL

He is an humble servant to Foible, my mother's woman, and may win her to your interest.

MIRABELL

Care is taken for that—she is won and worn by this time. They were married this morning.

MRS. FAINALL

Who?

MIRABELL

Waitwell and Foible. I would not tempt my servant to betray me by trusting him too far. If your mother, in hopes to ruin me, should consent to marry my pretended uncle, he might,

238 *lavish* licentious

like Mosca in *The Fox*, stand upon terms; so I made him sure beforehand.

MRS. FAINALL

So, if my poor mother is caught in a contract, you will discover the imposture betimes and release her, by producing a certificate of her gallant's former marriage.

MIRABELL

Yes, upon condition she consent to my marriage with her niece and surrender the moiety of her fortune in her possession.

MRS. FAINALL

She talked last night of endeavouring at a match between Millamant and your uncle.

MIRABELL

That was by Foible's direction, and my instruction, that she might seem to carry it more privately.

MRS. FAINALL

Well, I have an opinion of your success, for I believe my lady will do anything to get a husband, and when she has this which you have provided for her, I suppose she will submit to anything to get rid of him.

MIRABELL

Yes, I think the good lady would marry anything that resembled a man, though 'twere no more than what a butler could pinch out of a napkin.

MRS. FAINALL

Female frailty! We must all come to it, if we live to be old, and feel the craving of a false appetite when the true is decayed.

MIRABELL

An old woman's appetite is depraved like that of a girl—'tis the green sickness of a second childhood; and like the faint offer of a latter Spring, serves but to usher in the Fall, and withers in an affected bloom.

MRS. FAINALL

Here's your mistress.

Enter MRS. MILLAMANT, WITWOUD *and* MINCING

265 *condition she* Q1, Q2 (condition that she Ww)

260 *Mosca in The Fox*. In *Volpone* Mosca the parasite-servant refuses to deliver Volpone from judgement even when Volpone offers him half the spoils. Mosca wants all, and the result is that both he and Volpone fall (*Volpone*, V, xii).

284 *latter Spring*. Falstaff is called this by Prince Hal in *1 Henry IV*, I, ii, 152.

MIRABELL

Here she comes i'faith full sail, with her fan spread and her streamers out, and a shoal of fools for tenders—ha, no, I cry her mercy.

MRS. FAINALL

I see but one poor empty sculler, and he tows her woman after him. 290

MIRABELL

You seem to be unattended, madam. You used to have the *beau monde* throng after you, and a flock of gay fine perukes hovering round you.

WITWOUD

Like moths about a candle. I had like to have lost my comparison for want of breath! 295

MILLAMANT

Oh I have denied myself airs today. I have walked as fast through the crowd—

WITWOUD

As a favourite in disgrace; and with as few followers.

MILLAMANT

Dear Mr. Witwoud, truce with your similitudes; for I am as sick of 'em— 300

WITWOUD

As a physician of a good air—I cannot help it madam, though 'tis against myself.

MILLAMANT

Yet again! Mincing, stand between me and his wit.

WITWOUD

Do Mrs. Mincing, like a screen before a great fire. I confess I do blaze today, I am too bright. 305

MRS. FAINALL

But dear Millamant, why were you so long?

MILLAMANT

Long! Lord, have I not made violent haste? I have asked every living thing I met for you; I have enquired after you as after a new fashion. 310

287–8 *her streamers* Q1, Q2 (streamers Ww)
299 *in disgrace* Q1, Q2 (just disgraced Ww)

---

288 *streamers* ribbons, suggesting a flag-bedecked ship dressed overall and entering port; Dryden, *An Evening's Love*, II, i, has Wildblood marking Jacinta's entrance with 'Yonder she comes with full sails i'faith; I'll hail her amain for England.'

290 *sculler* a small boat rowed by a single oarsman

293 *peruke* wig

WITWOUD
Madam, truce with your similitudes! No, you met her husband and did not ask him for her.

MIRABELL
By your leave Witwoud, that were like enquiring after an old fashion, to ask a husband for his wife.

WITWOUD
Hum; a hit, a hit, a palpable hit, I confess it. 315

MRS. FAINALL
You were dressed before I came abroad.

MILLAMANT
Ay, that's true—oh but then I had—Mincing what had I? Why was I so long?

MINCING
Oh mem, your la'ship stayed to peruse a pecquet of letters.

MILLAMANT
Oh ay, letters—I had letters—I am persecuted with letters— 320
I hate letters—nobody knows how to write letters; and yet one has 'em, one does not know why. They serve one to pin up one's hair.

WITWOUD
Is that the way? Pray madam, do you pin up your hair with all your letters? I find I must keep copies. 325

MILLAMANT
Only with those in verse, Mr. Witwoud, I never pin up my hair with prose. I fancy one's hair would not curl if it were pinned up with prose. I think I tried once Mincing?

MINCING
Oh mem, I shall never forget it.

MILLAMANT
Ay, poor Mincing tift and tift all the morning. 330

MINCING
Till I had the cremp in my fingers I'll vow mem, and all to no purpose. But when your la'ship pins it up with poetry, it sits so pleasant the next day as anything and is so pure and so crips.

319 *pecquet* Q1 (pacquet Q2, Ww)
327–8 *I fancy . . . prose* Q1 (omitted Q2, Ww)
331 *cremp* Q1 (cramp Q2, Ww)

---

319 *pecquet* Mincing speaks affectedly.
330 *tift.* A usage in 1600 of this rare verb has the past perfect form 'tifted' (OED); it means 'prepare', 'make ready'.
334 *crips* obsolete form of 'crisp'

WITWOUD
Indeed, so crips?

MINCING
You're such a critic, Mr. Witwoud.

MILLAMANT
Mirabell, did not you take exceptions last night? Oh ay, and went away—now I think on't I'm angry—no, now I think on't I'm pleased—for I believe I gave you some pain.

MIRABELL
Does that please you?

MILLAMANT
Infinitely; I love to give pain.

MIRABELL
You would affect a cruelty which is not in your nature; your true vanity is in the power of pleasing.

MILLAMANT
Oh I ask your pardon for that—one's cruelty is one's power, and when one parts with one's cruelty one parts with one's power; and when one has parted with that, I fancy one's old and ugly.

MIRABELL
Ay, ay, suffer your cruelty to ruin the object of your power, to destroy your lover—and then how vain, how lost a thing you'll be! Nay, 'tis true; you are no longer handsome when you've lost your lover. Your beauty dies upon the instant; for beauty is the lover's gift; 'tis he bestows your charms: your glass is all a cheat. The ugly and the old, whom the looking-glass mortifies, yet after commendation can be flattered by it and discover beauties in it; for that reflects our praises rather than your face.

MILLAMANT
Oh the vanity of these men! Fainall, d'ye hear him? If they did not commend us, we were not handsome! Now you must know they could not commend one, if one was not handsome. Beauty the lover's gift! Lord, what is a lover, that it can give? Why, one makes lovers as fast as one pleases, and they live as long as one pleases, and they die as soon as one pleases; and then, if one pleases, one makes more.

WITWOUD
Very pretty. Why, you make no more of making of lovers, madam, than of making so many card-matches.

337 *did not* Q1, Q2 (did Ww)

365 *card-matches* matches made from cardboard

MILLAMANT

One no more owes one's beauty to a lover, than one's wit to an echo; they can but reflect what we look and say: vain empty things if we are silent or unseen, and want a being.

MIRABELL

Yet to those two vain empty things you owe two of the greatest pleasures of your life. 370

MILLAMANT

How so?

MIRABELL

To your lover you owe the pleasure of hearing yourselves praised, and to an echo the pleasure of hearing yourselves talk.

WITWOUD

But I know a lady that loves talking so incessantly she won't 375 give an echo fair play; she has that everlasting rotation of tongue, that an echo must wait till she dies before it can catch her last words.

MILLAMANT

Oh fiction! Fainall, let us leave these men.

MIRABELL (*Aside to* MRS. FAINALL)

Draw off Witwoud. 380

MRS. FAINALL

Immediately; I have a word or two for Mr. Witwoud.

MIRABELL

I would beg a little private audience too—

Exeunt WITWOUD *and* MRS. FAINALL

You had the tyranny to deny me last night, though you knew I came to impart a secret to you that concerned my love.

MILLAMANT

You saw I was engaged. 385

MIRABELL

Unkind. You had the leisure to entertain a herd of fools—things who visit you from their excessive idleness, bestowing on your easiness that time which is the incumbrance of their lives. How can you find delight in such society? It is impossible they should admire you, they are not capable; or if they 390 were, it should be to you as a mortification: so sure to please a fool is some degree of folly.

MILLAMANT

I please myself; besides, sometimes to converse with fools is for my health.

MIRABELL

Your health! Is there a worse disease than the conversation of fools?

MILLAMANT

Yes, the vapours; fools are physic for it next to assafoetida.

MIRABELL

You are not in a course of fools?

MILLAMANT

Mirabell, if you persist in this offensive freedom, you'll displease me. I think I must resolve after all not to have you—we shan't agree.

MIRABELL

Not in our physic, it may be.

MILLAMANT

And yet our distemper in all likelihood will be the same; for we shall be sick of one another. I shan't endure to be reprimanded nor instructed; 'tis so dull to act always by advice, and so tedious to be told of one's faults: I can't bear it. Well, I won't have you, Mirabell. I'm resolved—I think—you may go. Ha, ha, ha! What would you give, that you could help loving me?

MIRABELL

I would give something that you did not know I could not help it.

MILLAMANT

Come, don't look grave then. Well, what do you say to me?

MIRABELL

I say that a man may as soon make a friend by his wit, or a fortune by his honesty, as win a woman with plain dealing and sincerity.

MILLAMANT

Sententious Mirabell! Prithee don't look with that violent and inflexible wise face, like Solomon at the dividing of the child in an old tapestry hanging.

MIRABELL

You are merry, madam, but I would persuade you for one moment to be serious.

419–20 *one moment* Q1, Q2, W1 (a moment W2)

---

397 *assafoetida* a resinous gum with a strong alliacious odour, procured in Central Asia; used as an antispasmodic (OED)

398 *course of fools.* The company of fools is supposedly medicinal.

417 *Solomon* the episode of I Kings 3

MILLAMANT

What, with that face? No, if you keep your countenance, 'tis impossible I should hold mine. Well, after all, there is something very moving in a love-sick face—ha, ha, ha!—well I won't laugh; don't be peevish. Heigh-ho! Now I'll be melancholy, as melancholy as a watch-light. Well, Mirabell, if ever you will win me, woo me now. Nay, if you are so tedious, fare you well; I see they are walking away.

MIRABELL

Can you not find in the variety of your disposition one moment—

MILLAMANT

To hear you tell me that Foible's married, and your plot like to speed? No.

MIRABELL

But how you came to know it—

MILLAMANT

Unless by the help of the devil, you can't imagine, unless she should tell me herself. Which of the two it may have been, I will leave you to consider; and when you have done thinking of that, think of me. *Exit*

MIRABELL

I have something more—gone! Think of you! To think of a whirlwind, though 'twere in a whirlwind, were a case of more steady contemplation: a very tranquillity of mind and mansion. A fellow that lives in a windmill has not a more whimsical dwelling than the heart of a man that is lodged in a woman. There is no point of the compass to which they cannot turn, and by which they are not turned; and by one as well as another; for motion, not method, is their occupation. To know this, and yet continue to be in love, is to be made wise from the dictates of reason, and yet persevere to play the fool by the force of instinct. Oh here come my pair of turtles—what, billing so sweetly! Is not Valentine's Day over with you yet?

Enter WAITWELL *and* FOIBLE

Sirrah, Waitwell, why sure you think you were married for your own recreation, and not for my conveniency.

430 *that Foible's* Q1 (Foible's Q2, Ww)
433 *Unless by the help* Q1, Q2 (without the help Ww)

---

425 *watch-light* night-light

WAITWELL

Your pardon, sir. With submission, we have indeed been solacing in lawful delights; but still with an eye to business, sir. I have instructed her as well as I could. If she can take your directions as readily as my instructions, sir, your affairs are in a prosperous way.

MIRABELL

Give you joy, Mrs. Foible.

FOIBLE

Oh 'las sir, I'm so ashamed—I'm afraid my lady has been in a thousand inquietudes for me. But I protest, sir, I made as much haste as I could.

WAITWELL

That she did indeed, sir. It was my fault that she did not make more.

MIRABELL

That I believe.

FOIBLE

But I told my lady as you instructed me, sir, that I had a prospect of seeing Sir Rowland your uncle, and that I would put her ladyship's picture in my pocket to show him; which I'll be sure to say has made him so enamoured of her beauty, that he burns with impatience to lie at her ladyship's feet and worship the original.

MIRABELL

Excellent Foible! Matrimony has made you eloquent in love.

WAITWELL

I think she has profited, sir; I think so.

FOIBLE

You have seen Madam Millamant, sir?

MIRABELL

Yes.

FOIBLE

I told her, sir, because I did not know that you might find an opportunity; she had so much company last night.

MIRABELL

Your diligence will merit more—in the mean time—(*gives money*)

FOIBLE

Oh dear sir, your humble servant.

WAITWELL

Spouse.

471 *profited.* Waitwell parodies Puritan jargon.

MIRABELL

Stand off sir, not a penny—go on, and prosper, Foible; the lease shall be made good and the farm stocked, if we succeed.

FOIBLE

I don't question your generosity, sir; and you need not doubt of success. If you have no more commands sir, I'll be gone. I'm sure my lady is at her toilet, and can't dress till I come. Oh dear (*looking out*) I'm sure that was Mrs. Marwood that went by in a mask; if she has seen me with you I'm sure she'll tell my lady. I'll make haste home and prevent her. Your servant sir. B'w'y, Waitwell. *Exit* FOIBLE

WAITWELL

Sir Rowland if you please. The jade's so pert upon her preferment she forgets herself.

MIRABELL

Come sir, will you endeavour to forget yourself, and transform into Sir Rowland.

WAITWELL

Why sir, it will be impossible I should remember myself—married, knighted and attended all in one day! 'Tis enough to make any man forget himself. The difficulty will be how to recover my acquaintance and familiarity with my former self, and fall from my transformation to a reformation into Waitwell. Nay, I shan't be quite the same Waitwell neither—for now I remember me, I am married, and can't be my own man again.

Ay there's the grief; that's the sad change of life;
To lose my title and yet keep my wife. *Exeunt*

Act III, Scene i

A room in LADY WISHFORT'*s house*
LADY WISHFORT *at her toilet*, PEG *waiting*

LADY WISHFORT

Merciful, no news of Foible yet?

PEG

No madam.

499 *I am married* Q1 (I'm married Q2, Ww)

488 *B'w'y* God be with you
490 *preferment* promotion

LADY WISHFORT

I have no more patience. If I have not fretted myself till I am pale again, there's no veracity in me. Fetch me the red—the red, do you hear, sweetheart! An arrant ash colour, as I'm a person! Look you how this wench stirs! Why dost thou not fetch me a little red? Didst thou not hear me, Mopus?

PEG

The red ratafia does your ladyship mean, or the cherry brandy?

LADY WISHFORT

Ratafia, fool! No, fool! Not the ratafia, fool—grant me patience! I mean the Spanish paper, idiot! Complexion, darling. Paint, paint, paint! Dost thou understand that, changeling? Dangling thy hands like bobbins before thee! Why dost thou not stir, puppet? Thou wooden thing upon wires.

PEG

Lord, madam, your ladyship is so impatient. I cannot come at the paint, madam; Mrs. Foible has locked it up, and carried the key with her.

LADY WISHFORT

A pox take you both! Fetch me the cherry brandy then.

Exit PEG

I'm as pale and as faint, I look like Mrs. Qualmsick the curate's wife, that's always breeding. Wench, come, come, wench, what art thou doing, sipping? Tasting? Save thee, dost thou not know the bottle?

Enter PEG *with a bottle and china cup*

PEG

Madam, I was looking for a cup.

LADY WISHFORT

A cup! Save thee, and what a cup hast thou brought! Dost thou take me for a fairy, to drink out of an acorn? Why didst thou not bring thy thimble? Hast thou ne'er a brass thimble clinking in thy pocket with a bit of nutmeg? I warrant thee.

7 *Mopus* dull, stupid person 11 *Spanish paper* rouge

13 *changeling* an ugly or stupid child supposedly left by fairies in exchange for one stolen

27–8 *thimble . . . nutmeg* probably good-luck charms, but Swift, *Polite Conversation*, has Miss searching in her pocket for a thimble, and bringing out a nutmeg, which provokes the comment 'O Miss, have a care; for if you carry a Nutmeg in your Pocket, you'll certainly be married to an old Man'. (Ed. H. Davis and L. Landa [Oxford, 1957], p. 163.)

Come, fill, fill. So. Again. (*one knocks*) See who that is. Set down the bottle first. Here, here, under the table! What, wouldst thou go with the bottle in thy hand like a tapster? As I'm a person, this wench has lived in an inn upon the road before she came to me, like Maritornes the Asturian in *Don Quixote*. No Foible yet?

PEG

No madam; Mrs. Marwood.

LADY WISHFORT

Oh Marwood; let her come in. Come in, good Marwood.

Enter MRS. MARWOOD

MRS. MARWOOD

I'm surprised to find your ladyship in *déshabille* at this time of day.

LADY WISHFORT

Foible's a lost thing; has been abroad since morning, and never heard of since.

MRS. MARWOOD

I saw her but now, as I came masked through the park, in conference with Mirabell.

LADY WISHFORT

With Mirabell! You call my blood into my face with mentioning that traitor. She durst not have the confidence. I sent her to negotiate an affair, in which if I'm detected I'm undone. If that wheedling villain has wrought upon Foible to detect me, I'm ruined. Oh my dear friend, I'm a wretch of wretches if I'm detected.

MRS. MARWOOD

Oh madam, you cannot suspect Mrs. Foible's integrity.

LADY WISHFORT

Oh, he carries poison in his tongue that would corrupt integrity itself. If she has given him an opportunity, she has as good as put her integrity into his hands. Ah dear Marwood, what's integrity to an opportunity? Hark! I hear her. Go, you thing, and send her in.

Exit PEG

37 *déshabille* ed. (dishabilie Q1)

54 *Go, you thing, and send her in* placed at the end of Lady Wishfort's speech in Ww

---

33 *Maritornes* the innkeeper's daughter who takes part in the scene when Quixote is made a knight. Davis suggests Lady Wishfort would remember D'Urfey's popular play, Pt I, II, i.

Dear friend retire into my closet, that I may examine her with more freedom. You'll pardon me dear friend, I can make bold with you—there are books over the chimney—Quarles and Prynne, and the *Short View of the Stage*, with Bunyan's works, to entertain you.

Exit MRS. MARWOOD

Enter FOIBLE

Oh Foible, where hast thou been? What hast thou been doing?

FOIBLE

Madam, I have seen the party.

LADY WISHFORT

But what hast thou done?

FOIBLE

Nay, 'tis your ladyship has done, and are to do; I have only promised. But a man so enamoured—so transported! Well, here it is, all that is left ; [*shows picture*] all that is not kissed away. Well, if worshipping of pictures be a sin—poor Sir Rowland, I say.

LADY WISHFORT

The miniature has been counted like; but hast thou not betrayed me, Foible? Hast thou not detected me to that faithless Mirabell? What hadst thou to do with him in the park? Answer me: has he got nothing out of thee?

FOIBLE

So, the devil has been beforehand with me; what shall I say? [*Aside*] Alas, madam, could I help it, if I met that confident thing? Was I in fault? If you had heard how he used me, and

65–7 *Well, here it is . . . kissed away* (omitted Q2, Ww)

58 *Quarles*. Francis Quarles (1592–1644), author of the popular *Emblems, Divine and Moral* (1635) and of biblical narratives

58 *Prynne*. William Prynne wrote *Histrio-mastix*, a Puritan attack on the stage, in 1632.

58 *Short View*. Jeremy Collier's attack on the immorality and profaneness of the English stage came out two years before *The Way of the World* and included attacks on Congreve's earlier comedies.

59 *Bunyan's Works*. *Grace Abounding* (1666), *Pilgrim's Progress* (1678–79), *The Life and Death of Mr Badman* (1680), *The Holy War* (1682), reprinted frequently and very popular Puritan literature. Congreve mocked Puritans and their literature in his first play *The Old Bachelor*, where the merchant Fondlewife uses Puritan jargon and the gallant mocks *The Practice of Piety*. Lady Wishfort's taste in literature is suited to her view on the education of daughters, as expressed in Act V.

all upon your ladyship's account, I'm sure you would not suspect my fidelity. Nay, if that had been the worst, I could have borne; but he had a fling at your ladyship too—and then I could not hold; but, i'faith, I gave him his own!

LADY WISHFORT

Me? What did the filthy fellow say?

FOIBLE

Oh madam, 'tis a shame to say what he said—with his taunts and his fleers, tossing up his nose. Humh (says he), what, you are a-hatching some plot (says he), you are so early abroad, or catering (says he), ferreting, for some disbanded officer, I warrant. Half-pay is but thin subsistence (says he). Well, what pension does your lady propose? Let me see (says he), what, she must come down pretty deep now, she's superannuated (says he), and—

LADY WISHFORT

Ods my life, I'll have him, I'll have him murdered! I'll have him poisoned! Where does he eat? I'll marry a drawer to have him poisoned in his wine. I'll send for Robin from Locket's immediately.

FOIBLE

Poison him? Poisoning's too good for him. Starve him madam, starve him—marry Sir Rowland and get him disinherited! Oh you would bless yourself to hear what he said.

LADY WISHFORT

A villain. Superannuated!

FOIBLE

Humh (says he), I hear you are laying designs against me too (says he), and Mrs. Millamant is to marry my uncle; (he does not suspect a word of your ladyship); but (says he), I'll fit you for that I warrant you (says he), I'll hamper you for that (says he)—you and your old frippery too (says he), I'll handle you!

LADY WISHFORT

Audacious villain! Handle me! Would he durst! Frippery! Old frippery! Was there ever such a foul-mouthed fellow? I'll be married tomorrow, I'll be contracted tonight!

FOIBLE

The sooner the better madam.

84 *catering* procuring
90 *drawer* tavern-waiter, tapster
92 *Locket's* a famous eating house and tavern in Charing Cross
101 *fit* punish
102 *frippery* old ragged clothes

LADY WISHFORT

Will Sir Rowland be here, sayest thou? When, Foible?

FOIBLE

Incontinently madam. No new sheriff's wife expects the return of her husband after knighthood with that impatience, in which Sir Rowland burns for the dear hour of kissing your ladyship's hands after dinner.

LADY WISHFORT

Frippery! Superannuated frippery! I'll frippery the villain: I'll reduce him to frippery and rags! A tatterdemalion—I hope to see him hung with tatters, like a Long Lane penthouse, or a gibbet thief! A slander-mouthed railer! I warrant the spendthrift prodigal's in debt as much as the million lottery, or the whole court upon a birthday. I'll spoil his credit with his tailor! Yes, he shall have my niece with her fortune, he shall.

FOIBLE

He! I hope to see him lodge in Ludgate first, and angle into Blackfriars for brass farthings with an old mitten!

LADY WISHFORT

Ay dear Foible; thank thee for that, dear Foible. He has put me out of all patience. I shall never recompose my features to receive Sir Rowland with any economy of face. This wretch has fretted me that I am absolutely decayed—look, Foible.

112 *hands* Q1 (hand Q2, Ww)

---

109 *Incontinently* immediately

114 *tatterdemalion* ragged beggar

115–16 *Long Lane penthouse.* Long Lane ran from West Smithfield to the Barbican and was noted for its impudent rag-sellers. Their stalls may have been set up against the houses, with makeshift roofing, or the projecting upper stories of the wood-framed buildings may have provided their shelter; 'penthouse' can mean either projecting eaves or a makeshift shelter set up against a building.

117–18 *million lottery* the government lottery of 1694 (Davis)

118 *court . . . birthday.* The King's birthday was the occasion for wearing new clothes.

121 *Ludgate.* Ludgate Prison in Blackfriars held debtors, and the wretchedness of their condition was notorious.

121–2 *angle . . . mitten.* The prisoners would 'fish' for alms with a mitten let down on a line from upper windows to passers-by in the street. Brass farthings were the smallest units of money.

125 *economy* orderly arrangement

FOIBLE

Your ladyship has frowned a little too rashly indeed, madam. There are some cracks discernible in the white varnish.

LADY WISHFORT

Let me see the glass. Cracks, sayest thou? Why, I am arrantly flayed! I look like an old peeled wall! Thou must repair me Foible, before Sir Rowland comes, or I shall never keep up to my picture.

FOIBLE

I warrant you, madam. A little art once made your picture like you; and now a little of the same art must make you like your picture. Your picture must sit for you madam.

LADY WISHFORT

But art thou sure Sir Rowland will not fail to come? Or will a not fail when he does come? Will he be importunate, Foible, and push? For if he should not be importunate—I shall never break decorums—I shall die with confusion if I am forced to advance—oh no, I can never advance —I shall swoon if he should expect advances—no, I hope Sir Rowland is better bred, than to put a lady to the necessity of breaking her forms. I won't be too coy neither—I won't give him despair —but a little disdain is not amiss—a little scorn is alluring.

FOIBLE

A little scorn becomes your ladyship.

LADY WISHFORT

Yes, but tenderness becomes me best—a sort of a dyingness —you see that picture has a sort of a—ha, Foible? A swimminess in the eyes—yes, I'll look so—my niece affects it; but she wants features. Is Sir Rowland handsome? Let my toilet be removed; I'll dress above. I'll receive Sir Rowland here. Is he handsome? Don't answer me. I won't know. I'll be surprised. I'll be taken by surprise.

137–8 *will a not* Q1, Q2, W1 (will he not W2)
148–9 *swimminess* Q1 (swimmingness Q2, Ww)

---

131 *like an old peeled wall* reminiscent of Jonson, *Volpone*, I, v, 58–62:

MOSCA

. . . and those same hanging cheeks,
Couer'd with hide, in stead of skin: (nay, helpe, sir)
That looke like frozen dish-clouts, set on end.

CORVINO

Or, like an old smok'd wall, on which the raine
Ran downe in streakes.

FOIBLE

By storm, madam. Sir Rowland's a brisk man.

LADY WISHFORT

Is he! Oh then he'll importune, if he's a brisk man. I shall save decorums if Sir Rowland importunes. I have a mortal terror at the apprehension of offending against decorums. Nothing but importunity can surmount decorums. Oh I'm glad he's a brisk man. Let my things be removed, good Foible. *Exit*

Enter MRS. FAINALL

MRS. FAINALL

Oh Foible, I have been in a fright lest I should come too late. That devil Marwood saw you in the park with Mirabell, and I'm afraid will discover it to my lady.

FOIBLE

Discover what, madam?

MRS. FAINALL

Nay, nay, put not on that strange face. I am privy to the whole design, and know that Waitwell, to whom thou wert this morning married, is to personate Mirabell's uncle, and as such winning my lady, to involve her in those difficulties from which Mirabell only must release her, by his making his conditions to have my cousin and her fortune left to her own disposal.

FOIBLE

Oh dear madam, I beg your pardon. It was not my confidence in your ladyship that was deficient; but I thought the former good correspondence between your ladyship and Mr. Mirabell might have hindered his communicating this secret.

MRS. FAINALL

Dear Foible, forget that.

FOIBLE

Oh dear madam, Mr. Mirabell is such a sweet winning gentleman, but your ladyship is the pattern of generosity. Sweet lady, to be so good! Mr. Mirabell cannot choose but be grateful. I find your ladyship has his heart still. Now madam I can safely tell your ladyship our success. Mrs. Marwood had told my lady; but I warrant I managed myself. I turned it all for the better. I told my lady that Mr. Mirabell railed

158 *Nothing . . . decorums* omitted in Q2, Ww

154 *brisk* sprightly and licentious

at her. I laid horrid things to his charge, I'll vow; and my lady is so incensed, that she'll be contracted to Sir Rowland tonight, she says. I warrant I worked her up, that he may have her for asking for, as they say of a Welsh maidenhead.

MRS. FAINALL

Oh rare Foible!

FOIBLE

Madam, I beg your ladyship to acquaint Mr. Mirabell of his success. I would be seen as little as possible to speak to him—besides, I believe Madam Marwood watches me. She has a month's mind, but I know Mr. Mirabell can't abide her.

Enter FOOTMAN

John, remove my lady's toilet. Madam, your servant; my lady is so impatient, I fear she'll come for me if I stay.

MRS. FAINALL

I'll go with you up the back stairs lest I should meet her.

Exeunt

Enter MRS. MARWOOD

MRS. MARWOOD

Indeed, Mrs. Engine, is it thus with you? Are you become a go-between of this importance? Yes, I shall watch you. Why, this wench is the *passe-partout*, a very master-key to everybody's strongbox. My friend Fainall, have you carried it so swimmingly? I thought there was something in it; but it seems it's over with you. Your loathing is not from a want of appetite then, but from a surfeit, else you could never be so cool to fall from a principal to be an assistant: to procure for him! A pattern of generosity, that I confess. Well, Mr. Fainall, you have met with your match. Oh man, man! Woman, woman! The devil's an ass. If I were a painter, I would draw him like an idiot, a driveller, with a bib and bells. Man should have his head and horns, and woman the rest of him. Poor simple fiend! Madam Marwood has a month's mind, but he can't abide her! 'Twere better for him you had not been his confessor in that affair, without you could have kept his counsel closer. I shall not prove another pattern of generosity, and stalk for him till he takes his stand to aim at a fortune. He has not obliged me to that, with

214–15 *and stalk . . . fortune* (omitted Ww)

192–3 *a month's mind* a strong inclination
197 *Mrs. Engine* Mrs Trickery
209 *bells* an attribute of folly

those excesses of himself, and now I'll have none of him. Here comes the good lady, panting ripe, with a heart full of hope and a head full of care, like any chemist upon the day of projection.

Enter LADY WISHFORT

LADY WISHFORT

Oh dear Marwood, what shall I say for this rude forgetfulness? But my dear friend is all goodness. 220

MRS. MARWOOD

No apologies, dear madam. I have been very well entertained.

LADY WISHFORT

As I'm a person I am in a very chaos to think I should so forget myself—but I have such an *olio* of affairs really I know not what to do. (*calls*) Foible! I expect my nephew Sir Wilfull every moment too—why Foible?—he means to travel for improvement. 225

MRS. MARWOOD

Methinks Sir Wilfull should rather think of marrying than travelling at his years. I hear he is turned of forty. 230

LADY WISHFORT

Oh he's in less danger of being spoiled by his travels; I am against my nephews marrying too young. It will be time enough, when he comes back and has acquired discretion to choose for himself.

MRS. MARWOOD

Methinks Mrs. Millamant and he would make a very fit match. He may travel afterwards. 'Tis a thing very usual with young gentlemen. 235

LADY WISHFORT

I promise you I have thought on't; and since 'tis your judgement, I'll think on't again. I assure you I will; I value your judgement extremely. On my word, I'll propose it. 240

Enter FOIBLE

Come, come, Foible. I had forgot my nephew will be here before dinner, I must make haste.

FOIBLE

Mr. Witwoud and Mr. Petulant are come to dine with your ladyship.

219 *projection* the alchemist's final process for turning base metal into gold
225 *olio* a Spanish or Portuguese stew with a great variety of ingredients

LADY WISHFORT

Oh dear, I can't appear till I'm dressed. Dear Marwood, shall I be free with you again, and beg you to entertain 'em? I'll make all imaginable haste; dear friend excuse me. 245

Exeunt LADY WISHFORT *and* FOIBLE

Enter MRS. MILLAMANT *and* MINCING

MILLAMANT

Sure never anything was so inbred as that odious man. Marwood, your servant.

MRS. MARWOOD

You have a colour. What's the matter? 250

MILLAMANT

That horrid fellow Petulant has provoked me into a flame—I have broke my fan! Mincing, lend me yours. Is not all the powder out of my hair?

MRS. MARWOOD

No; what has he done?

MILLAMANT

Nay, he has done nothing; he has only talked; nay, he has said nothing neither; but he has contradicted everything that has been said. For my part, I thought Witwoud and he would have quarrelled. 255

MINCING

I vow mem, I thought once they would have fit

MILLAMANT

Well, 'tis a lamentable thing I'll swear, that one has not the liberty of choosing one's acquaintance as one does one's clothes. 260

MRS. MARWOOD

If we had the liberty, we should be as weary of one set of acquaintance, though never so good, as we are of one suit, though never so fine. A fool and a doily stuff would now and then find days of grace, and be worn for variety. 265

MILLAMANT

I could consent to wear 'em, if they would wear alike; but fools never wear out—they are such *drap-de-Berry* things,

260 *I'll swear* Q1 (I swear Q2, Ww)
263 *the liberty* Q1, Q2 (that liberty Ww)

---

259 *fit* Mincing's affected pronunciation for 'fought'
265 *doily* light woollen material for summer use
268 *drap-de-Berry* woollen cloth from Berry in France; of a coarse kind

without one could give 'em to one's chambermaid after a day or two!

MRS. MARWOOD

'Twere better so indeed. Or what think you of the playhouse? A fine gay glossy fool should be given there, like a new masking habit, after the masquerade is over and we have done with the disguise; for a fool's visit is always a disguise, and never admitted by a woman of wit but to blind her affair with a lover of sense. If you would but appear bare-faced now, and own Mirabell, you might as easily put off Petulant and Witwoud as your hood and scarf; and indeed 'tis time, for the town has found it; the secret is grown too big for the pretence. 'Tis like Mrs. Primly's great belly; she may lace it down before, but it burnishes on her hips. Indeed, Millamant, you can no more conceal it than my Lady Strammel can her face, that goodly face, which in defiance of her Rhenish wine tea will not be comprehended in a mask.

MILLAMANT

I'll take my death, Marwood, you are more censorious than a decayed beauty or a discarded toast. Mincing, tell the men they may come up. My aunt is not dressing. Their folly is less provoking than your malice.

Exit MINCING

The town has found it! What has it found? That Mirabell loves me is no more a secret, than it is a secret that you discovered it to my aunt, or than the reason why you discovered it is a secret.

MRS. MARWOOD

You are nettled.

MILLAMANT

You're mistaken. Ridiculous!

287 *dressing* Q1, Q2 (dressing here Ww)

---

273 *habit* costume

280 *Primly*. 'Prim' means affectedly strict, precise, or demure.

281 *burnish* grow plump

283 *Strammel* a lean, gaunt ill-favoured person or animal (OED)

284 *Rhenish wine tea*. Rhine wine was regarded as helpful in reducing corpulence and high colour (Summers, OED): but Davis thinks thin, hock-coloured tea may be meant.

286 *discarded toast* person fallen from popularity, whose health is no longer drunk

MRS. MARWOOD

Indeed my dear you'll tear another fan if you don't mitigate those violent airs.

MILLAMANT

Oh silly! Ha, ha, ha! I could laugh immoderately. Poor Mirabell! His constancy to me has quite destroyed his complaisance for all the world beside. I swear I never enjoined it him to be so coy. If I had the vanity to think he would obey me, I would command him to show more gallantry; 'tis hardly well-bred to be so particular on one hand, and so insensible on the other. But I despair to prevail, and so let him follow his own way. Ha, ha, ha! Pardon me, dear creature, I must laugh, ha, ha, ha! Though I grant you 'tis a little barbarous, ha, ha, ha!

MRS. MARWOOD

What pity 'tis, so much fine raillery, and delivered with so significant gesture, should be so unhappily directed to miscarry.

MILLAMANT

Ha? Dear creature, I ask your pardon; I swear I did not mind you.

MRS. MARWOOD

Mr. Mirabell and you both may think it a thing impossible, when I shall tell him, by telling you—

MILLAMANT

Oh dear, what? For it is the same thing, if I hear it—ha, ha, ha!

MRS. MARWOOD

That I detest him, hate him, madam.

MILLAMANT

Oh madam, why so do I—and yet the creature loves me, ha, ha, ha! How can one forbear laughing to think of it? I am a sybil if I am not amazed to think what he can see in me. I'll take my death, I think you are handsomer—and within a year or two as young. If you could but stay for me, I should overtake you—but that cannot be. Well, that thought makes me melancholy—now I'll be sad.

MRS. MARWOOD

Your merry note may be changed sooner than you think.

310 *Ha* ed. (Hae Q1, Q2, Ww)
323 *melancholy* Q1, Q2 (melancholic Ww)

---

319 *sybil* prophetess

MILLAMANT
D'ye say so. Then I'm resolved I'll have a song to keep up my spirits.

Enter MINCING

MINCING
The gentlemen stay but to comb, madam, and will wait on you.

MILLAMANT
Desire Mrs. —— that is in the next room to sing the song I would have learned yesterday. You shall hear it madam, not that there's any great matter in it, but 'tis agreeable to my humour.

SONG

Set by Mr. John Eccles, and sung by Mrs. Hodgson

I

Love's but the frailty of the mind
When 'tis not with ambition joined;
A sickly flame, which if not fed, expires;
And feeding, wastes in self-consuming fires.

II

'Tis not to wound a wanton boy
Or amorous youth, that gives the joy;
But 'tis the glory to have pierced a swain
For whom inferior beauties sighed in vain.

III

Then I alone the conquest prize
When I insult a rival's eyes:
If there's delight in love, 'tis when I see
That heart which others bleed for, bleed for me.

Enter PETULANT *and* WITWOUD

MILLAMANT
Is your animosity composed, gentlemen?

332 *and sung . . . Hodgson* Q1, Q2 (omitted Ww)

---

327 *comb.* Combing wigs was a customary masculine mode of conspicuous leisure.

332 *Mrs. Hodgson.* She had a high reputation as a singer and sang the part of Juno in *The Judgement of Paris*, for which Congreve much admired her.

WITWOUD

Raillery, raillery, madam, we have no animosity. We hit off a little wit now and then, but no animosity; the falling out of wits is like the falling out of lovers—we agree in the main like treble and bass. Ha, Petulant?

PETULANT

Ay, in the main, but when I have a humour to contradict. 350

WITWOUD

Ay, when he has a humour to contradict, then I contradict too. What, I know my cue. Then we contradict one another like two battledores: for contradictions beget one another like Jews.

PETULANT

If he says black's black—if I have a humour to say 'tis blue— 355
let that pass; all's one for that. If I have a humour to prove it, it must be granted.

WITWOUD

Not positively must—but it may—it may.

PETULANT

Yes it positively must, upon proof positive.

WITWOUD

Ay, upon proof positive it must; but upon proof presump- 360
tive it only may. That's a logical distinction now, madam.

MRS. MARWOOD

I perceive your debates are of importance and very learnedly handled.

PETULANT

Importance is one thing, and learning's another; but a debate's a debate, that I assert. 365

WITWOUD

Petulant's an enemy to learning; he relies altogether on his parts.

PETULANT

No, I'm no enemy to learning; it hurts not me.

MRS. MARWOOD

That's a sign indeed it's no enemy to you.

PETULANT

No, no, it's no enemy to anybody but them that have it. 370

MILLAMANT

Well, an illiterate man's my aversion. I wonder at the impudence of any illiterate man, to offer to make love.

353 *battledores* players striking a shuttlecock to and from each other, as in badminton

WITWOUD
That I confess I wonder at too.

MILLAMANT
Ah! To marry an ignorant, that can hardly read or write!

PETULANT
Why should a man be ever the further from being married though he can't read, any more than he is from being hanged? The Ordinary's paid for setting the psalm, and the parish priest for reading the ceremony; and for the rest which is to follow in both cases, a man may do it without book—so all's one for that.

MILLAMANT
D'ye hear the creature? Lord, here's company—I'll be gone.

Exeunt MILLAMANT *and* MINCING

WITWOUD
In the name of Bartlemew and his fair, what have we here?

MRS. MARWOOD
'Tis your brother, I fancy. Don't you know him?

WITWOUD
Not I—yes, I think it is he; I've almost forgot him; I have not seen him since the Revolution.

Enter SIR WILFULL WITWOUD *in a country riding habit, and* [*a*] SERVANT *to Lady Wishfort*

SERVANT
Sir, my lady's dressing. Here's company, if you please to walk in in the mean time.

SIR WILFULL
Dressing! What, it's but morning here, I warrant, with you in London. We should count it towards afternoon in our parts, down in Shropshire. Why then belike my aunt han't dined yet—ha, friend?

SERVANT
Your aunt, sir?

376 *any more than* Q1, Q2 (than Ww)

---

377 *Ordinary* the Newgate chaplain

382 *Bartlemew* the fair held on St Bartholomew's Day, 24 August, at Smithfield. Jonson's comedy of the same name exhibits some of the customary strange sights and alludes to others, such as the bull with five legs and two pizzles, which may be in Witwoud's mind as he gazes at Sir Wilfull.

385 *the Revolution* that of 1688 which brought William and Mary to the throne

SIR WILFULL

My aunt sir, yes my aunt sir, and your lady sir; your lady is my aunt sir! Why, what, dost thou not know me, friend? Why then send somebody here that does. How long hast thou lived with thy lady, fellow, ha?

SERVANT

A week sir: longer than anybody in the house except my lady's woman.

SIR WILFULL

Why then belike thou dost not know thy lady if thou seest her—ha, friend?

SERVANT

Why truly sir, I cannot safely swear to her face in a morning before she is dressed. 'Tis like I may give a shrewd guess at her by this time.

SIR WILFULL

Well, prithee try what thou canst do; if thou canst not guess, enquire her out, dost hear, fellow, and tell her her nephew, Sir Wilfull Witwoud, is in the house.

SERVANT

I shall sir.

SIR WILFULL

Hold ye—hear me friend, a word with you in your ear; prithee, who are these gallants?

SERVANT

Really sir, I can't tell; here come so many here, 'tis hard to know 'em all. *Exit*

SIR WILFULL

Oons, this fellow knows less than a starling; I don't think a' knows his own name.

MRS. MARWOOD

Mr. Witwoud, your brother is not behindhand in forgetfulness—I fancy he has forgot you, too.

WITWOUD

I hope so. The devil take him that remembers first, I say.

SIR WILFULL

Save you, gentlemen and lady.

MRS. MARWOOD

For shame Mr. Witwoud; why won't you speak to him? And you, sir?

395 *somebody here* Q1, Q2 (somebody hither Ww)
397 *anybody* Q1, Q2, W1 (any W2)

---

412 *Oons* corruption of the oath 'by God's wounds'

WITWOUD
Petulant, speak.

PETULANT
And you sir.

SIR WILFULL
No offence, I hope. (*salutes* MRS. MARWOOD)

MRS. MARWOOD
No, sure sir.

WITWOUD
This is a vile dog, I see that already. No offence! Ha, ha, ha, to him, to him, Petulant! Smoke him!

PETULANT
It seems as if you had come a journey, sir—hem, hem. (*surveying him round*)

SIR WILFULL
Very likely, sir, that it may seem so.

PETULANT
No offence, I hope, sir.

WITWOUD
Smoke the boots, the boots! Petulant, the boots! Ha, ha, ha!

SIR WILFULL
Maybe not sir; thereafter, as 'tis meant, sir.

PETULANT
I presume upon the information of your boots.

SIR WILFULL
Why 'tis like you may sir. If you are not satisfied with the information of my boots, sir, if you will step to the stable you may enquire further of my horse, sir!

PETULANT
Your horse, sir! Your horse is an ass, sir!

SIR WILFULL
Do you speak by way of offence, sir?

MRS. MARWOOD
The gentleman's merry, that's all sir—[*Aside*] 'slife, we shall have a quarrel betwixt an horse and an ass before they find one another out—you must not take anything amiss from your friends, sir. You are among your friends here, though it may be you don't know it. If I am not mistaken, you are Sir Wilfull Witwoud.

SIR WILFULL
Right, lady; I am Sir Wilfull Witwoud, so I write myself; no

422 *No offence* possibly reminiscent of Falstaff's attempts to excuse his insults to Hal (2 *Henry IV*, II, iv, 302, 5, 7) 'No abuse, Hal, o'mine honour,
429 *Smoke* mock

offence to anybody, I hope; and nephew to the Lady Wishfort of this mansion. 445

MRS. MARWOOD

Don't you know this gentleman, sir?

SIR WILFULL

Hum! What, sure 'tis not—yea, by'r Lady, but 'tis—'sheart I know not whether 'tis or no—yea but 'tis, by the Wrekin! Brother Anthony! What Tony i'faith! What, dost thou not know me? By'r Lady nor I thee, thou art so becravated and 450 beperiwigged! 'Sheart, why dost not speak? Art thou o'erjoyed?

WITWOUD

Odso brother, is it you? Your servant, brother.

SIR WILFULL

Your servant! Why, yours sir. Your servant again—'sheart, and your friend and servant to that—and a—(*puff*) and a 455 flapdragon for your service, sir! And a hare's foot, and a hare's scut for your service sir, an you be so cold and so courtly!

WITWOUD

No offence I hope, brother.

SIR WILFULL

'Sheart sir, but there is, and much offence! A pox, is this 460 your Inns o' Court breeding, not to know your friends and your relations, your elders and your betters?

WITWOUD

Why brother Wilfull of Salop, you may be as short as a Shrewsbury cake if you please, but I tell you 'tis not modish to know relations in town. You think you're in the country, 465 where great lubberly brothers slabber and kiss one another when they meet like a call of serjeants. 'Tis not the fashion here, 'tis not indeed, dear brother.

SIR WILFULL

The fashion's a fool, and you're a fop, dear brother. 'Sheart,

449 *Anthony* Q1, Q2 (Antony Ww)

---

448 *Wrekin* the prominent hill in Shropshire, a famous landmark

456 *flapdragon* a raisin which the players must snatch from burning brandy and extinguish by swallowing, in the game of the same name; clap or pox (Davis, citing *A Dictionary of the Canting Crew*)

457 *scut* tail

464 *Shrewsbury cake* a kind of shortcake, flat, round, crisp, made in Shrewsbury

467 *call of serjeants* a group of barristers who were all called to the bar (i.e. admitted to the profession) at the same time

I've suspected this. By'r Lady I conjectured you were a fop since you began to change the style of your letters, and write in a scrap of paper gilt round the edges, no broader than a *subpoena*. I might expect this, when you left off 'Honoured Brother,' and 'hoping you are in good health', and so forth, to begin with a 'Rat me, knight, I'm so sick of a last night's debauch'; 'ods heart, and then tell a familiar tale of a cock and a bull, and a whore and a bottle, and so conclude. You could write news before you were out of your time, when you lived with honest Pumplenose the attorney of Furnival's Inn: you could entreat to be remembered then to your friends round the Wrekin. We could have gazettes then, and *Dawks's Letter*, and the weekly bill, till of late days.

PETULANT

'Slife, Witwoud, were you ever an attorney's clerk? Of the family of the Furnivals? Ha, ha, ha!

WITWOUD

Ay, ay, but that was for a while. Not long, not long; pshaw, I was not in my own power then; an orphan, and this fellow was my guardian; ay, ay, I was glad to consent to that man to come to London. He had the disposal of me then. If I had not agreed to that, I might have been bound prentice to a felt-maker in Shrewsbury; this fellow would have bound me to a maker of felts!

SIR WILFULL

'Sheart, and better than to be bound to a maker of fops; where, I suppose, you have served your time, and now you may set up for yourself.

MRS. MARWOOD

You intend to travel, sir, as I'm informed.

SIR WILFULL

Belike I may, madam. I may chance to sail upon the salt seas, if my mind hold.

PETULANT

And the wind serve.

473 *subpoena* writ issued by Chancery commanding the presence of a defendant to answer the charge against him
475 *Rat me* corrupt form of the oath 'may God rot me'
479 *Pumplenose* i.e. pimplenose
480 *Furnival's Inn* a subordinate inn of court attached to Lincoln's Inn
481 *gazette* news sheet
482 *Dawks's Letter* a weekly news letter published in Great Carter Lane, St Paul's (Summers)
482 *weekly bill* recording deaths in the City of London

SIR WILFULL

Serve or not serve, I shan't ask licence of you, sir, nor the weathercock your companion. I direct my discourse to the lady, sir. 'Tis like my aunt may have told you, madam; yes, I have settled my concerns, I may say now, and am minded to see foreign parts, if and how the peace holds, whereby, that is, taxes abate.

MRS. MARWOOD

I thought you had designed for France at all adventures.

SIR WILFULL

I can't tell that; 'tis like I may, and 'tis like I may not; I am somewhat dainty in making a resolution, because when I make it, I keep it. I don't stand shill I, shall I, then; if I say't, I'll do't. But I have thoughts to tarry a small matter in town, to learn somewhat of your lingo first, before I cross the seas. I'd gladly have a spice of your French, as they say, whereby to hold discourse in foreign countries.

MRS. MARWOOD

Here is an academy in town for that use.

SIR WILFULL

There is? 'Tis like there may.

MRS. MARWOOD

No doubt you will return very much improved.

WITWOUD

Yes, refined, like a Dutch skipper from a whale-fishing.

Enter LADY WISHFORT *and* FAINALL

LADY WISHFORT

Nephew, you are welcome.

SIR WILFULL

Aunt, your servant.

FAINALL

Sir Wilfull, your most faithful servant.

SIR WILFULL

Cousin Fainall, give me your hand.

LADY WISHFORT

Cousin Witwoud, your servant; Mr. Petulant, your servant; nephew, you are welcome again. Will you drink anything after your journey, nephew, before you eat? Dinner's almost ready.

503 *peace* the Peace of Ryswick (1697) which halted the war with France; it was broken in 1701.

508 *shill I, shall I* shilly shally, undecided

516 *Dutch skipper*. The Dutch were proverbial for grossness.

SIR WILFULL

I'm very well I thank you, aunt; however, I thank you for your courteous offer. 'Sheart, I was afraid you would have been in the fashion too, and have remembered to have forgot your relations. Here's your cousin Tony, belike I mayn't call him brother for fear of offence.

LADY WISHFORT

Oh he's a rallier, nephew—my cousin's a wit, and your great wits always rally their best friends to choose. When you have been abroad, nephew, you'll understand raillery better. (FAINALL *and* MRS. MARWOOD *talk apart*)

SIR WILFULL

Why then let him hold his tongue in the mean time, and rail when that day comes.

Enter MINCING

MINCING

Mem, I come to acquaint your la'ship that dinner is impatient.

SIR WILFULL

Impatient? Why then belike it won't stay till I pull off my boots! Sweetheart, can you help me to a pair of slippers? My man's with his horses, I warrant.

LADY WISHFORT

Fie, fie, nephew, you would not pull off your boots here? Go down into the hall—dinner shall stay for you—my nephew's a little unbred, you'll pardon him, madam. Gentlemen, will you walk? Marwood—

MRS. MARWOOD

I'll follow you, madam—before Sir Wilfull is ready.

[*Exeunt all but* MRS. MARWOOD *and* FAINALL]

FAINALL

Why then Foible's a bawd, an arrant, rank, match-making bawd, and I, it seems, am a husband, a rank husband; and my wife a very arrant, rank wife—all in the way of the world. 'Sdeath, to be an anticipated cuckold, a cuckold in embryo! Sure I was born with budding antlers like a young satyr or a

535 *I come* Q1, Q2, W1 (I am come W2)
548 *an anticipated cuckold* Q1, Q2 (a cuckold by anticipation Ww)

---

531 *to choose* by choice, for preference
549 *satyr* having the head and body of a man and the ears, horns, tail, and legs of a goat

citizen's child! 'Sdeath, to be out-witted, to be out-jilted, out-matrimonied! If I had kept my speed like a stag, 'twere somewhat; but to crawl after, with my horns, like a snail, and outstripped by my wife! 'Tis scurvy wedlock! 550

MRS. MARWOOD

Then shake it off; you have often wished for an opportunity to part, and now you have it. But first, prevent their plot; the half of Millamant's fortune is too considerable to be parted with, to a foe—to Mirabell. 555

FAINALL

Damn him, that had been mine, had you not made that fond discovery; that had been forfeited, had they been married. My wife had added lustre to my horns by that increase of fortune; I could have worn 'em tipped with gold, though my forehead had been furnished like a deputy-lieutenant's hall. 560

MRS. MARWOOD

They may prove a cap of maintenance to you still, if you can away with your wife; and she's no worse than when you had her; I dare swear she had given up her game before she was married. 565

FAINALL

Hum, that may be; she might throw up her cards, but I'll be hanged if she did not put Pam in her pocket.

MRS. MARWOOD

You married her to keep you; and if you can contrive to have 570

552–3 *and outstripped* Q1 (and be outstripped Q2, Ww)
568–9 *she might . . . pocket* (omitted Ww)

---

550 *citizen's child* the joke about merchants, aldermen, and citizens being cuckolds was traditional; in *The Old Bachelor*, Bellmour remarks he must dub an alderman cuckold, 'that he may be of equal Dignity with the rest of his Brethren' (I, i, 159).

562–3 *deputy lieutenant's hall.* As second most prominent man in the county, the deputy lieutenant would have a grand house and the great hall had antlers on the walls; compare Jonson, *The Silent Woman*, IV, v, 111–13: 'but then he is so hung with pikes, halberds, peitronells, callivers, and muskets, that he lookes like a Iustice of peace's hall:'.

564 *cap of maintenance* 'a heraldic term for the kind of cap with two points like horns behind, borne in the arms of certain families' (Summers); the passage is reminiscent of the paradoxical witticisms of Touchstone on cuckoldom in *As You Like It*, III, iii, 42–54. Dr Johnson commented (on *Much Ado*, I, i, 208) 'Shakespeare had no mercy upon the poor cuckold, his horn is an inexhaustible subject of merriment'.

569 *Pam.* Jack of Clubs, highest card in the game of loo; Fainall implies that Mrs Fainall has kept Mirabell as an 'ace' up her sleeve.

her keep you better than you expected, why should you not keep her longer than you intended?

FAINALL

The means, the means.

MRS. MARWOOD

Discover to my lady your wife's conduct; threaten to part with her. My lady loves her, and will come to any composition to save her reputation. Take the opportunity of breaking it, just upon the discovery of this imposture. My lady will be enraged beyond bounds and sacrifice niece, and fortune, and all, at that conjuncture. And let me alone to keep her warm; if she should flag in her part I will not fail to prompt her.

FAINALL

Faith, this has an appearance.

MRS. MARWOOD

I'm sorry I hinted to my lady to endeavour a match between Millamant and Sir Wilfull; that may be an obstacle.

FAINALL

Oh, for that matter leave me to manage him; I'll disable him for that. He will drink like a Dane; after dinner I'll set his hand in.

MRS. MARWOOD

Well, how do you stand affected towards your lady?

FAINALL

Why faith I'm thinking of it. Let me see. I am married already, so that's over. My wife has played the jade with me. Well, that's over too. I never loved her, or if I had, why that would have been over too by this time. Jealous of her I cannot be, for I am certain; so there's an end of jealousy. Weary of her I am, and shall be. No, there's no end of that—no, no, that were too much to hope. Thus far concerning my repose. Now for my reputation. As to my own, I married not for it, so that's out of the question; and as to my part in my wife's, why, she had parted with hers before, so bringing none to me, she can take none from me. 'Tis against all rule of play that I should lose to one who has not wherewithal to stake.

MRS. MARWOOD

Besides you forget, marriage is honourable.

575–6 *composition* agreement
581 *appearance* i.e. of likely success
585 *Dane* proverbial for drunkenness
585–6 *set his hand in* start him off

FAINALL

Hum! Faith, and that's well thought on; marriage is honourable, as you say; and if so, wherefore should cuckoldom be a discredit, being derived from so honourable a root?

MRS. MARWOOD

Nay I know not; if the root be honourable, why not the branches?

FAINALL

So, so, why this point's clear. Well, how do we proceed?

MRS. MARWOOD

I will contrive a letter which shall be delivered to my lady at the time when that rascal who is to act Sir Rowland is with her. It shall come as from an unknown hand—for the less I appear to know of the truth, the better I can play the incendiary. Besides, I would not have Foible provoked if I could help it, because you know she knows some passages—nay I expect all will come out—but let the mine be sprung first, and then I care not if I'm discovered.

FAINALL

If the worst come to the worst, I'll turn my wife to grass. I have already a deed of settlement of the best part of her estate, which I wheedled out of her; and that you shall partake at least.

MRS. MARWOOD

I hope you are convinced that I hate Mirabell. Now you'll be no more jealous.

FAINALL

Jealous, no—by this kiss—let husbands be jealous; but let the lover still believe. Or, if he doubt, let it be only to endear his pleasure, and prepare the joy that follows, when he proves his mistress true. But let husbands' doubts convert to endless jealousy, or, if they have belief, let it corrupt to superstition and blind credulity. I am single, and will herd no more with 'em. True, I wear the badge, but I'll disown the order; and since I take my leave of 'em, I care not if I leave 'em a common motto to their common crest:

> All husbands must or pain, or shame, endure;
> The wise too jealous are, fools too secure.

Exeunt

616 *turn . . . to grass* (of horses) retire from service
627 *herd.* This metaphor concludes the imagery of horns.

Act IV, Scene i

Scene continues
Enter LADY WISHFORT *and* FOIBLE

LADY WISHFORT
Is Sir Rowland coming, sayest thou, Foible? And are things in order?

FOIBLE
Yes madam. I have put wax lights in the sconces, and placed the footmen in a row in the hall in their best liveries, with the coachman and postilion to fill up the equipage. 5

LADY WISHFORT
Have you pulvilled the coachman and postilion, that they may not stink of the stable when Sir Rowland comes by?

FOIBLE
Yes madam.

LADY WISHFORT
And are the dancers and the music ready, that he may be entertained in all points with correspondence to his passion? 10

FOIBLE
All is ready, madam.

LADY WISHFORT
And—well—and how do I look, Foible?

FOIBLE
Most killing well, madam.

LADY WISHFORT
Well, and how shall I receive him? In what figure shall I give his heart the first impression? There is a great deal in the first 15 impression. Shall I sit? No, I won't sit, I'll walk. Ay, I'll walk from the door upon his entrance, and then turn full upon him. No, that will be too sudden. I'll lie, ay, I'll lie down. I'll receive him in my little dressing-room, there's a couch—yes, yes, I'll give the first impression on a couch. I won't lie 20 neither, but loll and lean upon one elbow, with one foot a little dangling off, jogging in a thoughtful way. Yes; and then as soon as he appears, start, ay, start and be surprised, and rise to meet him in a pretty disorder. Yes. Oh, nothing is more alluring than a levee from a couch in some confusion; it shows 25

5 *fill up the equipage* complete the parade of all the staff
6 *pulvilled* sprinkled with perfumed powder
25 *levee* the action of rising from a bed or couch, usually associated with royalty; Lady Wishfort pretends to French sophistication and royal status.

the foot to advantage and furnishes with blushes and recomposing airs beyond comparison. Hark! There's a coach.

FOIBLE

'Tis he, madam.

LADY WISHFORT

Oh dear, has my nephew made his addresses to Millamant? I ordered him.

FOIBLE

Sir Wilfull is set in to drinking, madam, in the parlour.

LADY WISHFORT

Ods my life I'll send him to her. Call her down, Foible, bring her hither. I'll send him as I go. When they are together, then come to me Foible, that I may not be too long alone with Sir Rowland. *Exit*

Enter MRS. MILLAMANT *and* MRS. FAINALL

FOIBLE

Madam, I stayed here to tell your ladyship that Mr. Mirabell has waited this half hour for an opportunity to talk with you, though my lady's orders were to leave you and Sir Wilfull together. Shall I tell Mr. Mirabell that you are at leisure?

MILLAMANT

No. What would the dear man have? I am thoughtful and would amuse myself; bid him come another time.

There never yet was woman made
Nor shall, but to be cursed. (*repeating and walking about*)

That's hard.

MRS. FAINALL

You are very fond of Sir John Suckling today, Millamant, and the poets.

MILLAMANT

He? Ay, and filthy verses; so I am.

FOIBLE

Sir Wilfull is coming madam; shall I send Mr. Mirabell away?

MILLAMANT

Ay, if you please Foible, send him away—or send him hither—just as you will dear Foible. I think I'll see him—shall I? Ay, let the wretch come. [*Exit* FOIBLE]

Thyrsis a youth of the inspired train—(*repeating*)

42–3 *There never . . . cursed* the opening of an untitled poem by Sir John Suckling

52 *Thyrsis . . . train* the first line of Edmund Waller's *The Story of Phoebus and Daphne, Applied*

Dear Fainall, entertain Sir Wilfull; thou hast philosophy to undergo a fool, thou art married and hast patience. I would confer with my own thoughts.

MRS. FAINALL

I am obliged to you, that you would make me your proxy in this affair, but I have business of my own.

Enter SIR WILFULL

Oh Sir Wilfull, you are come at the critical instant. There's your mistress up to the ears in love and contemplation; pursue your point, now or never.

SIR WILFULL

Yes, my aunt would have it so. I would gladly have been encouraged with a bottle or two, because I'm somewhat wary at first, before I am acquainted. (*this while* MILLAMANT *walks about repeating to herself*) But I hope after a time I shall break my mind—that is, upon further acquaintance—so, for the present, cousin, I'll take my leave. If so be you'll be so kind to make my excuse, I'll return to my company.

MRS. FAINALL

Oh fie Sir Wilfull! What, you must not be daunted.

SIR WILFULL

Daunted? No, that's not it, it is not so much for that—for if so be that I set on't, I'll do't. But only for the present, 'tis sufficient till further acquaintance, that's all. Your servant.

MRS. FAINALL

Nay, I'll swear you shall never lose so favourable an opportunity if I can help it. I'll leave you together and lock the door. *Exit*

SIR WILFULL

Nay nay cousin—I have forgot my gloves—what d'ye do? 'Sheart! 'A has locked the door indeed, I think! Nay, cousin Fainall, open the door! Pshaw, what a vixen trick is this? Nay, now 'a has seen me too! Cousin, I made bold to pass through as it were—I think this door's enchanted!

MILLAMANT (*repeating*)

I prithee spare me, gentle boy,
Press me no more for that slight toy.

61 *would have* Q1 (will have Q2, Ww)

---

54 *undergo* endure

80 *I prithee* . . . the opening lines of another untitled Suckling poem; Millamant mocks Sir Wilfull with these ironically apt quotations.

SIR WILFULL
Anan? Cousin your servant.
MILLAMANT
That foolish trifle of a heart—
Sir Wilfull!
SIR WILFULL
Yes—your servant. No offence I hope, cousin.
MILLAMANT (*repeating*)
I swear it will not do its part
Though thou dost thine, employ'st thy power and art.
Natural, easy Suckling!
SIR WILFULL
Anan? Suckling? No such suckling neither, cousin, nor stripling; I thank heaven I'm no minor.
MILLAMANT
Ah rustic! Ruder than Gothic!
SIR WILFULL
Well, well, I shall understand your lingo one of these days, cousin; in the mean while I must answer in plain English.
MILLAMANT
Have you any business with me, Sir Wilfull?
SIR WILFULL
Not at present, cousin. Yes, I made bold to see, to come and know if that how you were disposed to fetch a walk this evening; if so be that I might not be troublesome, I would have sought a walk with you.
MILLAMANT
A walk? What then?
SIR WILFULL
Nay nothing—only for the walk's sake, that's all.
MILLAMANT
I nauseate walking, 'tis a country diversion. I loathe the country and everything that relates to it.

97 *sought* ed. (fought Q1, Q2)

---

87 *easy Suckling* a phrase of the Earl of Rochester's
88 *Suckling*. Sir Wilfull supposes Millamant is calling him a young calf or lamb.
90 *Gothic* barbarian; reminiscent of *As You Like It*, III, iii, 4–6: 'I am here with thee and thy goats, as the most capricious poet, honest Ovid, was among the Goths'
97 *sought*. Q has 'fought' which I take to be a misprint for 'sought' as does Davis; but Lynch prints 'fought' and notes it was a countrified version of 'fetched'.

SIR WILFULL

Indeed? Hah! Look ye, look ye, you do? Nay, 'tis like you may. Here are choice of pastimes here in town, as plays and the like—that must be confessed indeed—

MILLAMANT

Ah, *l'étourdie*! I hate the town too. 105

SIR WILFULL

Dear heart, that's much—hah!—that you should hate 'em both! Hah! 'Tis like you may; there are some can't relish the town, and others can't away with the country—'tis like you may be one of those, cousin.

MILLAMANT

Ha, ha, ha! Yes, 'tis like I may. You have nothing further to 110 say to me?

SIR WILFULL

Not at present, cousin; 'tis like, when I have an opportunity to be more private, I may break my mind in some measure—I conjecture you partly guess—however that's as time shall try; but spare to speak and spare to speed, as they say. 115

MILLAMANT

If it is of no great importance, Sir Wilfull, you will oblige me to leave me; I have just now a little business.

SIR WILFULL

Enough, enough, cousin, yes, yes, all a case; when you're disposed, when you're disposed. Now's as well as another time, and another time as well as now. All's one for that. Yes, 120 yes, if your concerns call you, there's no haste; it will keep cold, as they say. Cousin, your servant. I think this door's locked.

MILLAMANT

You may go this way sir.

SIR WILFULL

Your servant; then with your leave I'll return to my com- 125 pany. *Exit*

MILLAMANT

Ay, ay, ha, ha, ha!
Like Phoebus sung the no less am'rous boy.

Enter MIRABELL

119 *when you're disposed* (omitted W2)

---

105 *l'étourdie* the giddy town

127 *Like Phoebus* . . . the third line of the Waller poem previously quoted

MIRABELL

Like Daphne she, as lovely and as coy.
Do you lock yourself up from me, to make my search more curious? Or is this pretty artifice contrived, to signify that here the chase must end, and my pursuit be crowned, for you can fly no further?

MILLAMANT

Vanity! No. I'll fly and be followed to the last moment, though I am upon the very verge of matrimony; I expect you should solicit me as much as if I were wavering at the grate of a monastery, with one foot over the threshold. I'll be solicited to the very last, nay, and afterwards.

MIRABELL

What, after the last?

MILLAMANT

Oh, I should think I was poor and had nothing to bestow if I were reduced to an inglorious ease, and freed from the agreeable fatigues of solicitation.

MIRABELL

But do not you know that when favours are conferred upon instant and tedious solicitation that they diminish in their value, and that both the giver loses the grace and the receiver lessens his pleasure?

MILLAMANT

It may be in things of common application, but never sure in love. Oh, I hate a lover that can dare to think he draws a moment's air independent on the bounty of his mistress. There is not so impudent a thing in nature as the saucy look of an assured man, confident of success. The pedantic arrogance of a very husband has not so pragmatical an air. Ah, I'll never marry, unless I am first made sure of my will and pleasure.

MIRABELL

Would you have 'em both before marriage, or will you be

128 *Like Daphne* . . . Mirabell completes the couplet; compare *The Man of Mode* where Harriet completes Dorimant's couplet (*The Man of Mode*, V, ii, 92–3, ed. Brett-Smith [Oxford, 1927])

138 *What, after the last?* The proviso scene allows for a wide, lightly satiric survey of follies, affectations, and deceptions by partners in a marriage, reminiscent of Truewit's long speeches in II, ii, of Jonson's *The Silent Woman*, especially his warning 'euery halfe houres pleasure must be bought anew: and with the same paine, and charge, you woo'd her at first.'

151 *pragmatical* conceited

contented with the first now, and stay for the other till after grace?

MILLAMANT

Ah don't be impertinent. My dear liberty, shall I leave thee? My faithful solitude, my darling contemplation, must I bid you then adieu? Ay-h, adieu; my morning thoughts, agreeable wakings, indolent slumbers, all ye *douceurs*, ye *sommeils du matin*, adieu? I can't do't, 'tis more than impossible. Positively, Mirabell, I'll lie a-bed in a morning as long as I please.

MIRABELL

Then I'll get up in a morning as early as I please.

MILLAMANT

Ah, idle creature, get up when you will—and, d'ye hear, I won't be called names after I'm married; positively, I won't be called names.

MIRABELL

Names!

MILLAMANT

Ay, as wife, spouse, my dear, joy, jewel, love, sweetheart, and the rest of that nauseous cant in which men and their wives are so fulsomely familiar. I shall never bear that. Good Mirabell, don't let us be familiar or fond, nor kiss before folks like my Lady Fadler and Sir Francis, nor go to Hyde Park together the first Sunday in a new chariot, to provoke eyes and whispers, and then never to be seen there together again; as if we were proud of one another the first week, and ashamed of one another for ever after. Let us never visit together, nor go to a play together, but let us be very strange and well-bred; let us be as strange as if we had been married a great while, and as well-bred as if we were not married at all.

MIRABELL

Have you any more conditions to offer? Hitherto your demands are pretty reasonable.

175 *never to be* Q1, Q2 (never be Ww)
177 *for ever after* Q1 (ever after Q2, Ww)

---

170 *nauseous.* Like 'filthy', the word is not used with the strong emphasis it has today; affected exaggeration of such words ('dreadful', 'terrible', 'catastrophic') remains a characteristic of modern affected speech, however.

173 *Fadler* one who indulges in fondling

179 *strange* reserved

MILLAMANT

Trifles—as, liberty to pay and receive visits to and from whom I please, to write and receive letters, without interrogatories or wry faces on your part; to wear what I please, and choose conversation with regard only to my own taste; to have no obligation upon me to converse with wits that I don't like, because they are your acquaintance, or to be intimate with fools, because they may be your relations. Come to dinner when I please, dine in my dressing-room when I'm out of humour, without giving a reason. To have my closet inviolate, to be sole empress of my tea table, which you must never presume to approach without first asking leave; and lastly, wherever I am, you shall always knock at the door before you come in. These articles subscribed, if I continue to endure you a little longer, I may by degrees dwindle into a wife.

MIRABELL

Your bill of fare is something advanced in this latter account. Well, have I liberty to offer conditions, that when you are dwindled into a wife, I may not be beyond measure enlarged into a husband?

MILLAMANT

You have free leave; propose your utmost, speak and spare not.

MIRABELL

I thank you. *Imprimis* then, I covenant that your acquaintance be general; that you admit no sworn confidante or intimate of your own sex, no she-friend to screen her affairs under your countenance and tempt you to make trial of a mutual secrecy; no decoy-duck to wheedle you a fop, scrambling to the play in a mask, then bring you home in a pretended fright when you think you shall be found out, and rail at me for missing the play, and disappointing the frolic, which you had to pick me up and prove my constancy!

MILLAMANT

Detestable *imprimis*! I go to the play in a mask!

MIRABELL

Item, I article that you continue to like your own face as long as I shall, and while it passes current with me, that you

184 *visits* cf. Truewit: 'Then, you must keep what servants shee please; what company shee will; that friend must not visit you without her licence;'

205 *Imprimis* in the first place; a term used in legal contracts. What follows is reminiscent of *The Silent Woman*, II, ii, 99–105.

endeavour not to new-coin it. To which end, together with all vizards for the day, I prohibit all masks for the night made of oiled skins and I know not what—hog's bones, hare's gall, pig-water, and the marrow of a roasted cat. In short, I forbid all commerce with the gentlewoman in what-d'ye-call-it Court. *Item*, I shut my doors against all bawds with baskets, and pennyworth's of muslin, china, fans, atlases, etc. *Item*, when you shall be breeding—

MILLAMANT

Ah! Name it not.

MIRABELL

Which may be presumed, with a blessing on our endeavours—

MILLAMANT

Odious endeavours!

MIRABELL

I denounce against all strait-lacing, squeezing, for a shape, till you mould my boy's head like a sugar-loaf, and instead of a man-child make me the father to a crooked billet. Lastly, to the dominion of the tea table I submit, but with proviso that you exceed not in your province, but restrain yourself to native and simple tea table drinks, as tea, chocolate and coffee; as, likewise, to genuine and authorised tea table talk, such as mending of fashions, spoiling reputations, railing at absent friends, and so forth; but that on no account you encroach upon the men's prerogative and presume to drink healths or toast fellows; for prevention of which I banish all foreign forces, all auxiliaries to the tea table, as orange brandy, all aniseed, cinnamon, citron and Barbadoes waters, together with ratafia and the most noble spirit of clary. But, for cowslip wine, poppy water and all

231 *me the father* Q1, Q2 (me father Ww)

---

219 *hog's bones* reminiscent of *The Silent Woman*, II, ii, 137–9: 'lies in, a moneth, of a new face, all oyle, and birdlime; and rises in asses milke, and is clens'd with a new *fucus*:'

223 *atlases* rich silk-satin from the Orient, flowered with gold or silver (OED)

229 *strait-lacing* tightly-laced corsets

230 *sugar-loaf* moulded hard refined sugar, in a conical mass; also applied figuratively to a conical hill and the conical Tudor and Stuart tall hat

231 *billet* small stick

241 *orange brandy* brandy flavoured with orange-peel

242 *Barbadoes waters* brandy flavoured with orange and lemon peel

243 *clary* a drink made from brandy and clary flowers with the addition of sugar, cinnamon, and a little dissolved ambergris

dormitives, those I allow. These provisos admitted, in other things I may prove a tractable and complying husband. 245

MILLAMANT

Oh horrid provisos! Filthy strong waters! I toast fellows, odious men! I hate your odious provisos!

MIRABELL

Then we're agreed. Shall I kiss your hand upon the contract? And here comes one to be a witness to the sealing of the deed. 250

Enter MRS. FAINALL

MILLAMANT

Fainall, what shall I do? Shall I have him? I think I must have him.

MRS. FAINALL

Ay, ay, take him, take him, what should you do?

MILLAMANT

Well then—I'll take my death I'm in a horrid fright—Fainall, I shall never say it—well—I think—I'll endure you. 255

MRS. FAINALL

Fie, fie, have him, have him, and tell him so in plain terms; for I am sure you have a mind to him.

MILLAMANT

Are you? I think I have; and the horrid man looks as if he thought so too. Well, you ridiculous thing you, I'll have you —I won't be kissed, nor I won't be thanked—here, kiss my 260 hand though—so, hold your tongue now, and don't say a word.

MRS. FAINALL

Mirabell, there's a necessity for your obedience: you have neither time to talk nor stay. My mother is coming, and, in my conscience, if she should see you, would fall into fits and 265 maybe not recover time enough to return to Sir Rowland, who as Foible tells me is in a fair way to succeed. Therefore, spare your ecstasies for another occasion and slip down the back stairs, where Foible waits to consult you.

MILLAMANT

Ay, go, go. In the mean time I suppose you have said 270 something to please me.

261 *and don't* Q1, Q2 (don't Ww)

---

244 *dormitives* drinks to induce sleep

MIRABELL

I am all obedience. *Exit*

MRS. FAINALL

Yonder Sir Wilfull's drunk, and so noisy that my mother has been forced to leave Sir Rowland to appease him; but he answers her only with singing and drinking. What they have done by this time I know not, but Petulant and he were upon quarrelling as I came by.

MILLAMANT

Well, if Mirabell should not make a good husband, I am a lost thing, for I find I love him violently.

MRS. FAINALL

So it seems, when you mind not what's said to you. If you doubt him, you had best take up with Sir Wilfull.

MILLAMANT

How can you name that superannuated lubber? Foh!

Enter WITWOUD *from drinking*

MRS. FAINALL

So, is the fray made up, that you have left 'em?

WITWOUD

Left 'em? I could stay no longer. I have laughed like ten christenings; I am tipsy with laughing. If I had stayed any longer I should have burst, I must have been let out and pieced in the sides like an unsized camlet! Yes, yes, the fray is composed; my lady came in like a *nolle prosequi* and stopped their proceedings.

MILLAMANT

What was the dispute?

WITWOUD

That's the jest, there was no dispute, they could neither of 'em speak for rage, and so fell a-sputtering at one another like two roasting apples.

Enter PETULANT *drunk*

275 *they have* Q1, Q2 (they may have Ww)
280 *when you* Q1, Q2 (for you Ww)
289 *their proceedings* Q1, Q2 (the proceedings Ww)

---

287 *pieced* enlarged with pieces of inserted material
287 *unsized camlĕt* unstiffened material, originally rich and Oriental, but subsequently a debased shoddy imitation
288 *nolle prosequi* term for ending legal proceedings

Now Petulant, all's over, all's well; Gad, my head begins to whim it about! Why dost thou not speak? Thou art both as drunk and as mute as a fish.

PETULANT

Look you Mrs. Millamant, if you can love me, dear nymph—say it—and that's the conclusion; pass on, or pass off—that's all.

WITWOUD

Thou hast uttered volumes, folios, in less than *decimo sexto*, my dear Lacedemonian, Sirrah Petulant: thou art an epitomiser of words.

PETULANT

Witwoud, you are an annihilator of sense.

WITWOUD

Thou art a retailer of phrases, and dost deal in remnants of remnants, like a maker of pincushions. Thou art in truth (metaphorically speaking) a speaker of shorthand.

PETULANT

Thou art (without a figure) just one half of an ass; and Baldwin yonder, thy half-brother, is the rest. A gemini of asses split would make just four of you.

WITWOUD

Thou dost bite, my dear mustard seed; kiss me for that.

PETULANT

Stand off! I'll kiss no more males; I have kissed your twin yonder in a humour of reconciliation till he (*hiccup*) rises upon my stomach like a radish.

MILLAMANT

Eh! Filthy creature! What was the quarrel?

PETULANT

There was no quarrel. There might have been a quarrel.

WITWOUD

If there had been words enow between 'em to have expressed

295 *whim it about* spin

300 *decimo sexto* a book of very small size in which each sheet is folded into sixteen leaves (whereas a folio is composed of sheets folded into two leaves)

301 *Lacedemonian*. Spartan brevity is Petulant's gift.

308 *Baldwin* an ass in the beast epic *Reynard the Fox* reprinted in 1694 (Davis)

308 *gemini* pair of twins

313 *radish* perhaps reminiscent of Sir Toby's difficulties with pickled herring in *Twelfth Night*, I, v, 114

provocation they had gone together by the ears like a pair of castanets.

PETULANT

You were the quarrel.

MILLAMANT

Me! 320

PETULANT

If I have a humour to quarrel, I can make less matters conclude premises. If you are not handsome, what then, if I have a humour to prove it? If I shall have my reward, say so; if not, fight for your face the next time yourself—I'll go sleep.

WITWOUD

Do, wrap thyself up like a woodlouse and dream revenge! 325 And hear me, if thou canst learn to write by tomorrow morning, pen me a challenge: I'll carry it for thee.

PETULANT

Carry your mistress's monkey a spider! Go flea dogs, and read romances! I'll go to bed to my maid. *Exit*

MRS. FAINALL

He's horridly drunk. How came you all in this pickle? 330

WITWOUD

A plot, a plot, to get rid of the knight; your husband's advice; but he sneaked off.

Enter LADY [WISHFORT] *and* SIR WILFULL *drunk*

LADY WISHFORT

Out upon't, out upon't, at years of discretion, and comport yourself at this rantipole rate?

SIR WILFULL

No offence, aunt. 335

LADY WISHFORT

Offence! As I'm a person I'm ashamed of you—fogh! How

325 *woodlouse* reminiscent of *The Silent Woman*, II, iv, 140–42: 'Or a snaile, or a hog-louse: I would roule my selfe vp for this day, introth, they should not vnwinde me.'

328 *Carry . . . spider* bawdy, as in Marston, *The Malcontent* (ed. Bernard Harris, 1968) I, iii, 40–41:

PIETRO

How dost thou live nowadays, Malevole?

MALEVOLE

Why, like the knight, Sir Patrick Penlolians, with killing of spiders for my lady's monkey.

334 *rantipole* grossly ill-mannered

you stink of wine! D'ye think my niece will ever endure such a borachio? You're an absolute borachio!

SIR WILFULL

Borachio!

LADY WISHFORT

At a time when you should commence an amour and put your best foot foremost— 340

SIR WILFULL

'Sheart, an you grutch me your liquor, make a bill—give me more drink, and take my purse! (*sings*)

Prithee fill me the glass
Till it laugh in my face 345
With ale that is potent and mellow;
He that whines for a lass
Is an ignorant ass,
For a bumper has not its fellow.

But if you would have me marry my cousin, say the word and I'll do't; Wilfull will do't, that's the word; Wilfull will do't, that's my crest; my motto I have forgot. 350

LADY WISHFORT

My nephew's a little overtaken, cousin, but 'tis with drinking your health; o' my word you are obliged to him.

SIR WILFULL

In vino veritas, aunt. If I drunk your health today, cousin, I am a borachio! But, if you have a mind to be married, say the word, and send for the piper, Wilfull will do't. If not, dust it away, and let's have t'other round. Tony! Ods heart where's Tony? Tony's an honest fellow, but he spits after a bumper, and that's a fault. (*sings*) 355 360

We'll drink and we'll never ha' done boys,
Put the glass then around with the sun boys,
Let Apollo's example invite us;
For he's drunk every night
And that makes him so bright 365
That he's able next morning to light us.

345 *laugh* Q1, Ww (laughs Q2)

---

338 *borachio* the Spanish leathern bottle for wine, hence the term for drunkard and the name of the minor character in *Much Ado About Nothing*

342 *grutch* begrudge

349 *bumper* brim-full glass of wine

355 *In vino veritas* drunkards speak the truth

The sun's a good pimple, an honest soaker, he has a cellar at your Antipodes. If I travel, aunt, I touch at your Antipodes—your Antipodes are a good rascally sort of topsy-turvy fellows—if I had a bumper I'd stand upon my head and drink a health to 'em. A match or no match, cousin with the hard name? Aunt, Wilfull will do't: if she has her maidenhead let her look to't; if she has not, let her keep her own counsel in the meantime, and cry out at the nine months' end.

MILLAMANT

Your pardon madam, I can stay no longer—Sir Wilfull grows very powerful—egh! How he smells! I shall be overcome if I stay. Come, cousin.

Exeunt MILLAMANT *and* MRS. FAINALL

LADY WISHFORT

Smells! He would poison a tallow chandler and his family. Beastly creature, I know not what to do with him. Travel, quotha! Ay, travel, travel, get thee gone, get thee but far enough, to the Saracens, or the Tartars, or the Turks, for thou art not fit to live in a Christian commonwealth, thou beastly pagan!

SIR WILFULL

Turks? no, no Turks, aunt; your Turks are infidels, and

367 *pimple* good companion

368 *Antipodes* perhaps reminiscent of *Much Ado*, II, i, 234–40. Popular notions about men who lived upside down on the other side of the world derive principally from Mandeville's *Voyages*, a source for the play *The Antipodes* by Richard Brome (1638) in which the question is posed

> what people
> Are they of the Antipodes? Are they not such
> As Mandeville writes of, without heads or necks,
> Having their eyes plac'd on their shoulders, and
> Their mouths amidst their breasts? (I, vi, 98–102, ed. A. Haaker, 1967)

In this play Peregrine has become mad with reading traveller's tales, and is deluded that he is in the Antipodes, where he finds such topsy-turvy marvels as aldermen who love poetry and honest lawyers. Sir Wilfull, as the embodiment of saturnalian spirit in the play, and a would-be traveller, is appropriately associated with Brome's play and his Peregrine.

377 *smells* Millamant finds Sir Wilfull's insinuations as repellent as his smell; he smells personally and metaphorically.

379 *tallow chandler* maker of tallow candles; Sir Fopling objects to their smell: 'How can you breathe in a Room where there's Grease frying!' (*Man of Mode*, IV, i, 283).

believe not in the grape. Your Mahometan, your Mussulman, is a dry stinkard—no offence, aunt. My map says that your Turk is not so honest a man as your Christian; I cannot find by the map that your Mufti is orthodox; whereby it is a plain case, that orthodox is a hard word, aunt, and (*hiccup*) Greek for claret. (*sings*)

To drink is a Christian diversion,
Unknown to the Turk and the Persian;
Let Mahometan fools
Live by heathenish rules
And be damned over tea cups and coffee!
But let British lads sing,
Crown a health to the king,
And a fig for your sultan and sophy!

Ah Tony!

Enter FOIBLE, *and whispers* LADY [WISHFORT]

LADY WISHFORT

Sir Rowland impatient? Good lack! What shall I do with this beastly tumbril? Go lie down and sleep, you sot, or as I'm a person I'll have you bastinadoed with broomsticks! Call up the wenches. *Exit* FOIBLE

SIR WILFULL

Ahey! Wenches! Where are the wenches?

LADY WISHFORT

Dear cousin Witwoud, get him away, and you will bind me to you inviolably. I have an affair of moment that invades me with some precipitation. You will oblige me to all futurity.

WITWOUD

Come, knight. Pox on him, I don't know what to say to him. Will you go to a cock-match?

393 *Turk and* Q1, Q2 (Turk or Ww)
404 *wenches* Q1, Q2 (wenches with broomsticks Ww)

---

387 *dry* teetotal
389 *Mufti.* Mohammedan priest
391 *Greek* Jaques in *As You Like It,* II, v, 54–5 describes 'ducdame' as a 'Greek invocation, to call fools into a circle'.
402 *tumbril* heavy cart
403 *bastinadoed* beaten on the soles of the feet, or, simply, punished with a beating
410 *cock-match* cock-fight

SIR WILFULL

With a wench, Tony? Is she a shake-bag, sirrah? Let me bite your cheek for that.

WITWOUD

Horrible! He has a breath like a bagpipe. Ay, ay, come, will you march, my Salopian?

SIR WILFULL

Lead on little Tony—I'll follow thee my Anthony, my Tantony; sirrah, thou shalt be my Tantony, and I'll be thy pig— 415

And a fig for your sultan and sophy.

Exit singing with WITWOUD

LADY WISHFORT

This will never do. It will never make a match—at least before he has been abroad. 420

Enter WAITWELL *disguised as for Sir Rowland*

Dear Sir Rowland, I am confounded with confusion at the retrospection of my own rudeness. I have more pardons to ask than the Pope distributes in the year of Jubilee; but I hope where there is likely to be so near an alliance, we may unbend the severity of decorum, and dispense with a little ceremony. 425

WAITWELL

My impatience, madam, is the effect of my transport; and till

411 *shake-bag* game-cock, the largest and strongest kind of fighting-cock and able to give any opponent a good fight

414 *Salopian.* Shropshire man

416–17 *Tantony . . . pig.* The point of the jest is in the contrast between Witwoud's thinness and Sir Wilfull's fatness (compare *2 Henry IV*, I, ii, 12–14 where Falstaff says to his boy 'I do here walk before thee like a sow that hath overwhelm'd all her litter but one'). There are contradictory associations in the term Tantony pig, since in religious art St Anthony has a pig as an attribute to mark his triumph over gluttony and the devil. The Hospital Brothers of St Anthony of Clermont had a privileged herd of pigs famous for their fatness; a Tantony pig could be a very large pig, therefore. On the other hand it could mean the smallest pig in a litter, proverbial for obsequiousness; if this is the sense, Sir Wilfull jestingly reverses the obvious application to Witwoud; but the more likely sense is that of extra fatness.

418 *sophy* the name of the Persian dynasty of Shahs was Sufi

423 *year of Jubilee* a year in which the Pope proclaimed remission of punishments imposed for sin: 1700, the year of the play's first performance, was a Jubilee Year: but there had been a much talked-of Jubilee in 1691, alluded to in Farquhar's play *The Constant Couple: or, a Trip to the Jubilee* (1699).

I have the possession of your adorable person, I am tantalized on a rack, and do but hang, madam, on the tenter of expectation.

LADY WISHFORT

You have excess of gallantry Sir Rowland, and press things to a conclusion with a most prevailing vehemence. But a day or two for decency of marriage—

WAITWELL

For decency of funeral, madam. The delay will break my heart—or, if that should fail, I shall be poisoned. My nephew will get an inkling of my designs and poison me—and I would willingly starve him before I die—I would gladly go out of the world with that satisfaction. That would be some comfort to me, if I could but live so long as to be revenged on that unnatural viper.

LADY WISHFORT

Is he so unnatural, say you? Truly I would contribute much both to the saving of your life and the accomplishment of your revenge; not that I respect myself, though he has been a perfidious wretch to me.

WAITWELL

Perfidious to you!

LADY WISHFORT

Oh Sir Rowland, the hours that he has died away at my feet, the tears that he has shed, the oaths that he has sworn, the palpitations that he has felt, the trances, and the tremblings, the ardours and the ecstasies, the kneelings and the risings, the heart-heavings and the hand-grippings, the pangs and the pathetic regards of his protesting eyes, oh no memory can register!

WAITWELL

What, my rival! Is the rebel my rival? 'A dies!

LADY WISHFORT

No, don't kill him at once Sir Rowland, starve him gradually, inch by inch.

WAITWELL

I'll do't. In three weeks he shall be barefoot; in a month out at knees with begging an alms. He shall starve upward and

428 *a rack* Q1 (the rack Q2, Ww)

---

428 *tenter* associated with suspense or tension. The tenter was a wooden frame with hooks on which cloth was stretched after milling so that it would dry without distortion or shrinking.

439 *viper*. In the Aesop fable the viper stung the husbandman who nursed it.

upward, till he has nothing living but his head, and then go out in a stink, like a candle's end upon a save-all.

LADY WISHFORT

Well, Sir Rowland, you have the way; you are no novice in the labyrinth of love, you have the clue. But, as I am a person, Sir Rowland, you must not attribute my yielding to any sinister appetite, or indigestion of widowhood, nor impute my complacency to any lethargy of continence. I hope you do not think me prone to any iteration of nuptials— 460 465

WAITWELL

Far be it from me—

LADY WISHFORT

If you do, I protest I must recede—or think that I have made a prostitution of decorums, but in the vehemence of compassion, and to save the life of a person of so much importance— 470

WAITWELL

I esteem it so—

LADY WISHFORT

Or else you wrong my condescension—

WAITWELL

I do not, I do not—

LADY WISHFORT

Indeed you do—

WAITWELL

I do not, fair shrine of virtue— 475

LADY WISHFORT

If you think the least scruple of carnality was an ingredient—

WAITWELL

Dear madam, no. You are all camphire and frankincense, all chastity and odour—

464 *iteration* ed. (interation Q1, Q2)

---

458 *save-all* a small metal dish with a pin projecting from the centre on which the candle end was fixed so that the candle burned right to the end

462 *sinister appetite.* Lady Wishfort's cumbrous circumlocutions all amount to the same claim: that sexual desire is not a motive in her agreement to marry.

478 *camphire.* Camphor was supposed to lessen desire.

478 *frankincense* an aromatic gum resin from the tree *Boswellia*; 'frank' seems to have originally meant 'valuable' (OED).

LADY WISHFORT
Or that— 480

Enter FOIBLE

FOIBLE
Madam, the dancers are ready, and there's one with a letter who must deliver it into your own hands.

LADY WISHFORT
Sir Rowland, will you give me leave? Think favourably, judge candidly, and conclude you have found a person who would suffer racks in honour's cause, dear Sir Rowland, and 485 will wait on you incessantly. *Exit*

WAITWELL
Fie, fie, what a slavery have I undergone! Spouse, hast thou any cordial—I want spirits.

FOIBLE
What a washy rogue art thou, to pant thus for a quarter of an hour's lying and swearing to a fine lady! 490

WAITWELL
Oh, she is the antidote to desire. Spouse, thou wilt fare the worse for't. I shall have no appetite to iteration of nuptials this eight and forty hours! By this hand, I'd rather be a chairman in the dog-days than act Sir Rowland, till this time tomorrow. 495

Enter LADY WISHFORT *with a letter*

LADY WISHFORT
Call in the dancers. Sir Rowland, we'll sit if you please and see the entertainment.

Dance

Now with your permission Sir Rowland I will peruse my letter. I would open it in your presence, because I would not make you uneasy. If it should make you uneasy I would 500 burn it. Speak if it does—but you may see by the superscription it is like a woman's hand.

FOIBLE [*Aside to* WAITWELL]
By heaven! Mrs. Marwood's, I know it. My heart aches! Get it from her!

501–2 *by the superscription it is like* Q1, Q2 (the superscription is like Ww)

---

489 *washy* wishy-washy, weak

493–4 *chairman in the dog-days* sedan-chair bearer in the hottest days of summer. Two men carried the completely enclosed chair in which the passenger sat.

WAITWELL

A woman's hand? No madam, that's no woman's hand, I see that already: that's somebody whose throat must be cut.

LADY WISHFORT

Nay Sir Rowland, since you give me a proof of your passion by your jealousy, I promise you I'll make you a return, by a frank communication. You shall see it. We'll open it together. Look you here. (*reads*) 'Madam, though unknown to you'—look you there, 'tis from nobody that I know—'I have that honour for your character, that I think myself obliged to let you know you are abused. He who pretends to be Sir Rowland is a cheat and a rascal'—
Oh heavens! What's this?

FOIBLE

Unfortunate. All's ruined.

WAITWELL

How, how? Let me see, let me see! (*reading*) 'A rascal and disguised and suborned for that imposture'—oh villainy! Oh villainy!—'by the contrivance of'—

LADY WISHFORT

I shall faint, I shall die, I shall die! Oh!

FOIBLE [*Aside to* WAITWELL]

Say 'tis your nephew's hand—quickly, his plot—swear, swear it!

WAITWELL

Here's a villain! Madam, don't you perceive it, don't you see it?

LADY WISHFORT

Too well, too well. I have seen too much.

WAITWELL

I told you at first I knew the hand. A woman's hand? The rascal writes a sort of a large hand, your Roman hand. I saw there was a throat to be cut presently! If he were my son—as he is my nephew—I'd pistol him!

FOIBLE

Oh treachery! But are you sure, Sir Rowland, it is his writing?

520 *I shall die, I shall die! Oh!* Q1 (I shall die! Oh! Q2, Ww)

527 *Roman hand* round and bold handwriting; perhaps reminiscent of Malvolio (*Twelfth Night*, III, iv, 29) insinuating to Olivia that he recognises her as the author of the letter commending his yellow stockings: 'I think we do know the sweet Roman hand'

WAITWELL

Sure? Am I here? Do I live? Do I lose this pearl of India? I have twenty letters in my pocket from him in the same character.

LADY WISHFORT

How!

FOIBLE

Oh what luck it is Sir Rowland that you were present at this juncture! This was the business that brought Mr. Mirabell disguised to Madam Millamant this afternoon. I thought something was contriving when he stole by me and would have hid his face.

LADY WISHFORT

How, how! I heard the villain was in the house, indeed, and now I remember, my niece went away abruptly when Sir Wilfull was to have made his addresses.

FOIBLE

Then, then madam, Mr. Mirabell waited for her in her chamber; but I would not tell your ladyship to discompose you when you were to receive Sir Rowland.

WAITWELL

Enough! His date is short.

FOIBLE

No, good Sir Rowland, don't incur the law.

WAITWELL

Law? I care not for law. I can but die, and 'tis in a good cause. My lady shall be satisfied of my truth and innocence, though it cost me my life.

LADY WISHFORT

No, dear Sir Rowland, don't fight, if you should be killed I must never show my face; or hanged—oh consider my reputation, Sir Rowland! No, you shan't fight. I'll go in and examine my niece; I'll make her confess. I conjure you Sir Rowland, by all your love, not to fight.

WAITWELL

I am charmed, madam; I obey. But some proof you must let me give you. I'll go for a black box which contains the writings of my whole estate, and deliver that into your hands.

LADY WISHFORT

Ay, dear Sir Rowland, that will be some comfort; bring the black box.

534 *character* style of handwriting

547 *His date is short.* He dies shortly.

WAITWELL

And may I presume to bring a contract to be signed this night? May I hope so far?

LADY WISHFORT

Bring what you will; but come alive, pray come alive. Oh, this is a happy discovery!

WAITWELL

Dead or alive I'll come, and married we will be in spite of treachery; ay, and get an heir that shall defeat the last remaining glimpse of hope in my abandoned nephew. Come, my buxom widow!

Ere long you shall substantial proof receive
That I'm an arrant knight—

FOIBLE [*Aside*] Or arrant knave. *Exeunt*

Act V, Scene i

Scene continues
Enter LADY WISHFORT *and* FOIBLE

LADY WISHFORT

Out of my house, out of my house, thou viper, thou serpent that I have fostered! Thou bosom traitress, that I raised from nothing, begone, begone, begone! Go! Go! That I took from washing of old gauze and weaving of dead hair, with a bleak blue nose, over a chafing dish of starved embers, and

572 *an arrant knight* punning on the phrase 'knight-errant' and 'arrant' = 'knavish'

1 *viper*. The serpent stung the husbandman who nursed it. Lady Wishfort's tirade has close connections with the flyting match between Subtle and Face in Jonson, *The Alchemist*, I, i, 25–110; see Subtle's taunt

> Thou vermine, haue I tane thee, out of dung,
> So poore, so wretched, when no liuing thing
> Would keepe thee companie, but a spider, or worse?
> Rais'd thee from broomes, and dust, and watring pots?

4 *gauze* thin transparent fabric, silk linen or cotton

4 *weaving of dead hair* making wigs

5 *bleak blue nose*. Face taunts Subtle with finding him

> at *pie-corner*,
> Taking your meale of steeme in, from cookes stalls,
> Where, like the father of hunger, you did walke
> Piteously costiue, with your pinch'd-horne-nose (25–8).

5 *chafing dish* vessel holding burning coal to warm dishes placed on it

dining behind a traverse rag, in a shop no bigger than a birdcage! Go, go, starve again! Do! Do!

FOIBLE

Dear madam, I'll beg pardon on my knees.

LADY WISHFORT

Away, out, out! Go set up for yourself again! Do, drive a trade, do! With your threepennyworth of small ware, flaunting upon a packthread, under a brandy-seller's bulk, or against a dead wall by a ballad-monger! Go hang out an old frisoneer gorget, with a yard of yellow colberteen again, do! An old gnawed mask, two rows of pins and a child's fiddle, a glass necklace with the beads broken, and a quilted nightcap with one ear! Go, go, drive a trade! These were your commodities, you treacherous trull, this was your merchandise you dealt in, when I took you into my house, placed you next myself, and made you governante of my whole family. You have forgot this, have you, now you have feathered your nest?

FOIBLE

No, no, dear madam. Do but hear me, have but a moment's patience, I'll confess all. Mr. Mirabell seduced me. I am not the first that he has wheedled with his dissembling tongue. Your ladyship's own wisdom has been deluded by him; then how should I, a poor ignorant, defend myself? Oh madam, if you knew but what he promised me, and how he assured me your ladyship should come to no damage; or else the wealth of the Indies should not have bribed me to conspire

17–18 *your merchandise* Q1, Q2 (the merchandise Ww)

---

6 *traverse rag* tattered curtain

11 *flaunting upon a packthread.* The phrase 'upon a packthread' could be analogous to 'on a shoestring' and packthread certainly has associations of poverty and toughness: carriers, heavy bundles. However, the phrase most probably means: 'displaying yourself impudently on a drum of packthread', though the OED records Middleton, *The Black Book*: 'apparelled in villainous packthread'. Lady Wishfort implies that Foible would offer more than her small ware for sale.

11 *bulk* stall

12 *dead wall* a continuous wall, with the suggestion of monotony, dreariness, slum areas

12 *ballad-monger* a beggarly occupation

13 *frisoneer gorget* stiff neckpiece (French, *gorge*, throat) made of Friesland stuff

13 *colberteen* cheap lace

19 *governante* housekeeper

against so good, so sweet, so kind a lady as you have been to me.

LADY WISHFORT

No damage? What, to betray me, to marry me to a cast servingman? To make me a receptacle, an hospital for a decayed pimp? No damage? Oh thou frontless impudence—more than a big-bellied actress!

FOIBLE

Pray do but hear me madam, he could not marry your ladyship, madam, no indeed. His marriage was to have been void in law, for he was married to me first, to secure your ladyship. He could not have bedded your ladyship; for if he had consummated with your ladyship he must have run the risk of the law and been put upon his clergy. Yes indeed; I enquired of the law in that case before I would meddle or make.

LADY WISHFORT

What, then I have been your property, have I? I have been convenient to you, it seems, while you were catering for Mirabell. I have been broker for you! What, have you made a passive bawd of me? This exceeds all precedent; I am brought to fine uses, to become a botcher of secondhand marriages between Abigails and Andrews! I'll couple you, yes, I'll baste you together, you and your Philander! I'll Duke's Place you, as I'm a person! Your turtle is in custody already: you shall coo in the same cage, if there be constable or warrant in the parish! *Exit*

FOIBLE

Oh that ever I was born, oh that I was ever married! A bride, ay, I shall be a Bridewell bride! Oh!

Enter MRS. FAINALL

51 *constable* Q1, Q2, W1 (a constable W2)

---

34 *frontless* shameless

41 *put upon his clergy.* A criminal who could read and write might claim 'benefit of clergy' to escape the death penalty (Lynch).

42 *meddle or make* co-operate

45 *broker* second-hand dealer, hence procurer, pimp, bawd

48 *Abigails and Andrews* maidservants and manservants

49 *baste* flog

49 *Philander* lover

49–50 *Duke's Place* irregular marriages were notorious at St James's Church there

54 *Bridewell* the London prison where beating hemp was a punishment for women prisoners

MRS. FAINALL

Poor Foible, what's the matter?

FOIBLE

Oh madam, my lady's gone for a constable; I shall be had to a justice, and put to Bridewell to beat hemp. Poor Waitwell's gone to prison already.

MRS. FAINALL

Have a good heart, Foible, Mirabell's gone to give security for him; this is all Marwood's and my husband's doing.

FOIBLE

Yes, yes, I know it madam. She was in my lady's closet, and overheard all that you said to me before dinner. She sent the letter to my lady, and that missing effect, Mr. Fainall laid this plot to arrest Waitwell when he pretended to go for the papers; and in the mean time Mrs. Marwood declared all to my lady.

MRS. FAINALL

Was there no mention made of me in the letter? My mother does not suspect my being in the confederacy? I fancy Marwood has not told her, though she has told my husband.

FOIBLE

Yes madam, but my lady did not see that part—we stifled the letter before she read so far. Has that mischievous devil told Mr. Fainall of your ladyship then?

MRS. FAINALL

Ay, all's out, my affair with Mirabell, everything, discovered. This is the last day of our living together, that's my comfort.

FOIBLE

Indeed madam, and so 'tis a comfort if you knew all. He has been even with your ladyship; which I could have told you long enough since, but I love to keep peace and quietness by my good will; I had rather bring friends together than set 'em at distance. But Mrs. Marwood and he are nearer related than ever their parents thought for.

MRS. FAINALL

Say'st thou so, Foible? Canst thou prove this?

FOIBLE

I can take my oath of it, madam, so can Mrs. Mincing. We have had many a fair word from Madam Marwood, to conceal something that passed in our chamber one evening when you were at Hyde Park, and we were thought to have gone a-walking. But we went up unawares, though we were sworn to secrecy too. Madam Marwood took a book and swore us upon it; but it was but a book of verses and poems, so as long as it was not a Bible oath, we may break it with a safe conscience.

MRS. FAINALL

This discovery is the most opportune thing I could wish. Now Mincing?

Enter MINCING

MINCING

My lady would speak with Mrs. Foible, mem. Mr. Mirabell is with her; he has set your spouse at liberty, Mrs. Foible, and would have you hide yourself in my lady's closet, till my old lady's anger is abated. Oh, my old lady is in a perilous passion at something Mr. Fainall has said; he swears, and my old lady cries. There's a fearful hurricane, I vow. He says, mem, how that he'll have my lady's fortune made over to him, or he'll be divorced.

MRS. FAINALL

Does your lady and Mirabell know that?

MINCING

Yes mem, they have sent me to see if Sir Wilfull be sober, and to bring him to them. My lady is resolved to have him I think, rather than lose such a vast sum as six thousand pound. Oh come Mrs. Foible, I hear my old lady.

MRS. FAINALL

Foible, you must tell Mincing that she must prepare to vouch when I call her.

FOIBLE

Yes, yes, madam.

MINCING

Oh yes mem, I'll vouch anything for your ladyship's service, be what it will. *Exeunt* MINCING *and* FOIBLE

Enter LADY WISHFORT *and* MRS. MARWOOD

LADY WISHFORT

Oh my dear friend, how can I enumerate the benefits that I have received from your goodness? To you I owe the timely discovery of the false vows of Mirabell; to you the detection of the impostor Sir Rowland. And now you are become an intercessor with my son-in-law, to save the honour

89 *verses and poems* Q1, Q2 (poems Ww)
89–90 *as long as* Q1 (long as Q2, Ww)
102 *lady and* Q1, Q2 (lady or Ww)
114–15 *to you the detection* Q1, Q2 (to you I owe the detection Ww)

of my house, and compound for the frailties of my daughter. Well, friend, you are enough to reconcile me to the bad world, or else I would retire to deserts and solitudes, and feed harmless sheep by groves and purling streams. Dear Marwood, let us leave the world, and retire by ourselves and be shepherdesses.

MRS. MARWOOD

Let us first dispatch the affair in hand, madam, we shall have leisure to think of retirement afterwards. Here is one who is concerned in the treaty.

LADY WISHFORT

Oh daughter, daughter, is it possible thou shouldst be my child, bone of my bone and flesh of my flesh, and, as I may say, another me, and yet transgress the most minute particle of severe virtue? Is it possible you should lean aside to iniquity, who have been cast in the direct mould of virtue? I have not only been a mould but a pattern for you, and a model for you, after you were brought into the world.

MRS. FAINALL

I don't understand your ladyship.

LADY WISHFORT

Not understand? Why, have you not been naught? Have you not been sophisticated? Not understand? Here I am ruined to compound for your caprices and your cuckoldoms; I must pawn my plate, and my jewels, and ruin my niece, and all little enough—

MRS. FAINALL

I am wronged and abused, and so are you. 'Tis a false accusation, as false as hell, as false as your friend there, ay or your friend's friend, my false husband.

MRS. MARWOOD

My friend, Mrs. Fainall? Your husband my friend? What do you mean?

MRS. FAINALL

I know what I mean, madam, and so do you, and so shall the world at a time convenient.

MRS. MARWOOD

I am sorry to see you so passionate, madam. More temper would look more like innocence; but I have done. I am sorry my zeal to serve your ladyship should admit of misconstruction, or make me liable to affronts. You will pardon me,

117 *compound* settle by making concessions
134 *naught* lewd
135 *sophisticated* corrupted

madam, if I meddle no more with an affair in which I am not personally concerned.

LADY WISHFORT

Oh dear friend, I am so ashamed that you should meet with such returns;—[*to* MRS. FAINALL] you ought to ask pardon on your knees, ungrateful creature! She deserves more from you than all your life can accomplish. [*to* MRS. MARWOOD] Oh, don't leave me destitute in this perplexity! No, stick to me, my good genius.

MRS. FAINALL

I tell you madam you're abused! Stick to you? Ay, like a leech, to suck your best blood—she'll drop off when she's full. Madam, you sha' not pawn a bodkin, nor part with a brass counter, in composition for me! I defy 'em all; let 'em prove their aspersions, I know my own innocence, and dare stand by a trial. *Exit*

LADY WISHFORT

Why, if she should be innocent, if she should be wronged after all, ha? I don't know what to think—and I promise you, her education has been unexceptionable—I may say it, for I chiefly made it my own care to initiate her very infancy in the rudiments of virtue, and to impress upon her tender years a young odium and aversion to the very sight of men. Ay, friend, she would ha' shrieked if she had but seen a man, till she was in her teens; as I'm a person, 'tis true! She was never suffered to play with a male child, though but in coats; nay her very babies were of the feminine gender. Oh, she never looked a man in the face but her own father, or the chaplain —and him we made a shift to put upon her for a woman, by the help of his long garments and his sleek face—till she was going in her fifteen.

MRS. MARWOOD

'Twas much she should be deceived so long.

LADY WISHFORT

I warrant you, or she would never have borne to have been catechised by him, and have heard his long lectures against singing and dancing and such debaucheries, and going to

160 *sha' not* Q1 (shan't Q2, Ww)
163 *stand by* Q1, Q2 (stand Ww)

---

160 *bodkin* ornamental hairpin
161 *brass counter* very small and insignificant sum of money
173 *babies* dolls
175 *made a shift to put upon her* contrived to present to her

filthy plays, and profane music-meetings, where the lewd trebles squeak nothing but bawdy, and the basses roar blasphemy. Oh, she would have swooned at the sight or name of an obscene playbook! And can I think, after all this, that my daughter can be naught? What, a whore, and thought it excommunication to set her foot within the door of a playhouse? Oh my dear friend, I can't believe it, no, no; as she says, let him prove it, let him prove it.

MRS. MARWOOD

Prove it madam? What, and have your name prostituted in a public court! Yours and your daughter's reputation worried at the bar by a pack of bawling lawyers? To be ushered in with an Oyez of scandal, and have your case opened by an old fumbling lecher, in a quoif like a man midwife; to bring your daughter's infamy to light, to be a theme for legal punsters and quibblers by the statute, and become a jest, against a rule of court, where there is no precedent for a jest in any record, not even in Doomsday Book; to discompose the gravity of the bench, and provoke naughty interrogatories in more naughty law Latin, while the good judge, tickled with the proceeding, simpers under a grey beard and fidges off and on his cushion, as if he had swallowed cantharides, or sat upon cow-itch.

LADY WISHFORT

Oh, 'tis very hard.

MRS. MARWOOD

And then to have my young revellers of the Temple take

188 *Oh my dear* Q1, Q2 (Oh dear Ww)

190 *Prove it.* The recital of the miseries of going to law which Mrs. Marwood here begins owes much to the similar performance of Truewit on the miseries of marriage in *The Silent Woman,* II, ii.

193 *Oyez* the cry 'hear ye' used by court criers to gain silence for proclamations

194 *quoif* a white cap then worn by barristers

198 *Doomsday Book.* William the Conqueror's census and survey of his new kingdom, compiled in 1085–86; proverbially used to mean 'remote history'.

199 *naughty* lewd

201 *simpers* smirks, leers

201 *fidges* fidgets

202 *cantharides* a compound of dried beetles (Spanish Fly) thought to be aphrodisiac because of its irritant property

203 *cow-itch* the stinging hairs of the pods of a tropical plant

205 *of the Temple* i.e. students of the Inns of Court

notes like prentices at a conventicle, and after talk it all over again in commons, or before drawers in an eating house.

LADY WISHFORT

Worse and worse.

MRS. MARWOOD

Nay this is nothing; if it would end here, 'twere well; but it must after this be consigned by the shorthand writers to the public press, and from thence be transferred to the hands, nay into the throats and lungs of hawkers, with voices more licentious than the loud flounder-man's, or the woman that cries grey peas! And this you must hear till you are stunned —nay, you must hear nothing else for some days!

LADY WISHFORT

Oh, 'tis insupportable! No, no, dear friend, make it up, make it up; ay, ay, I'll compound. I'll give up all, myself and my all, my niece and her all—anything, everything, for composition!

MRS. MARWOOD

Nay madam, I advise nothing, I only lay before you as a friend the inconveniences which perhaps you have overseen. Here comes Mr. Fainall. If he will be satisfied to huddle up all in silence, I shall be glad. You must think I would rather congratulate than condole with you.

Enter FAINALL

LADY WISHFORT

Ay, ay, I do not doubt it, dear Marwood; no, no, I do not doubt it.

FAINALL

Well madam, I have suffered myself to be overcome by the

206 *all over* Q1, Q2 (over Ww)

---

206 *prentices . . . conventicle.* Dissenting tradesmen customarily required their apprentices to take notes during sermons for the later edification of their families; the connections between Puritanism and economic individualism in the period are discussed by Ian Watt in *The Rise of the Novel* (London, 1952).

207 *commons* meals in hall

213 *flounder-man's.* Etherege's Harriet in *The Man of Mode*, V, ii, 433–4, says 'There's musick in the worst Cry in *London*! *My Dill and Cowcumbers to pickle*!' Summers notes that a famous crier of flounders flourished from William and Mary to the end of George I's reign and his 'tones, in lengthening out the word flounders, were so happily varied, that people heard him with surprise and some degree of pleasure'.

221 *overseen* overlooked

importunity of this lady your friend, and am content you shall enjoy your own proper estate during life, on condition you oblige yourself never to marry, under such penalty as I think convenient.

LADY WISHFORT

Never to marry?

FAINALL

No more Sir Rowlands; the next imposture may not be so timely detected.

MRS. MARWOOD

That condition, I dare answer, my lady will consent to without difficulty; she has already but too much experienced the perfidiousness of men. Besides madam, when we retire to our pastoral solitude we shall bid adieu to all other thoughts.

LADY WISHFORT

Ay that's true; but in case of necessity, as of health, or some such emergency—

FAINALL

Oh, if you are prescribed marriage, you shall be considered; I will only reserve to myself the power to choose for you. If your physic be wholesome, it matters not who is your apothecary. Next, my wife shall settle on me the remainder of her fortune not made over already, and for her maintenance depend entirely on my discretion.

LADY WISHFORT

This is most inhumanly savage, exceeding the barbarity of a Muscovite husband.

FAINALL

I learned it from his Czarish majesty's retinue, in a winter evening's conference over brandy and pepper, amongst other secrets of matrimony and policy, as they are at present

248 *Muscovite husband.* Peter the Great visited London in 1697, which perhaps refreshed English attitudes to Russian matrimonial customs, formed by Elizabethan travellers' accounts. Anthony Jenkinson, for instance, in 1558, wrote: 'When they are going to bedde, the bridegrome putteth certain money, both golde and silver, if he have it, into one of his boots and then sitteth down in the chamber, crossing his legges, and then the bride must plucke off one of his boots . . . if she misse the boot wherein the money is, she doth not only loose the money, but is also bound from that day forwards to pull of his boots continually . . . one common rule is amongst them, if the woman be not beaten with the whip once a weeke, she will not be good, and therefore they looke for it orderly, & the women say, that if their husbands did not beate them, they should not love them.' (*Hakluyt's Voyages*[Glasgow, 1903], II, 446).

practised in the northern hemisphere. But this must be agreed unto, and that positively. Lastly, I will be endowed in right of my wife with that six thousand pound which is the moiety of Mrs. Millamant's fortune in your possession, and which she has forfeited (as will appear by the last will and testament of your deceased husband Sir Jonathan Wishfort) by her disobedience in contracting herself against your consent or knowledge, and by refusing the offered match with Sir Wilfull Witwoud, which you, like a careful aunt, had provided for her.

LADY WISHFORT

My nephew was *non compos*, and could not make his addresses.

FAINALL

I come to make demands—I'll hear no objections.

LADY WISHFORT

You will grant me time to consider.

FAINALL

Yes, while the instrument is drawing to which you must set your hand, till more sufficient deeds can be perfected; which I will take care shall be done with all possible speed. In the mean while, I will go for the said instrument, and till my return you may balance this matter in your own discretion. *Exit* FAINALL

LADY WISHFORT

This insolence is beyond all precedent, all parallel! Must I be subject to this merciless villain?

MRS. MARWOOD

'Tis severe indeed, madam, that you should smart for your daughter's wantonness.

LADY WISHFORT

'Twas against my consent that she married this barbarian, but she would have him, though her year was not out. Ah, her first husband, my son Languish, would not have carried it thus. Well, that was my choice, this is hers; she is matched now with a witness! I shall be mad, dear friend, is there no comfort for me? Must I live to be confiscated at this rebel rate? Here come two more of my Egyptian plagues, too.

262 *non compos* not in his right mind
266 *instrument* document
277 *her year* her year's mourning for her first husband
280 *with a witness* emphatic phrase, equivalent to 'with a vengeance' (Lynch)
281 *rebel* extortionate
282 *Egyptian plagues* see Exodus 7–12. Ten plagues visited the Pharaoh.

Enter MILLAMANT *and* SIR WILFULL

SIR WILFULL

Aunt, your servant.

LADY WISHFORT

Out, caterpillar, call not me aunt, I know thee not.

SIR WILFULL

I confess I have been a little in disguise as they say; 'sheart, and I'm sorry for't. What would you have? I hope I committed no offence, aunt, and if I did I am willing to make satisfaction: and what can a man say fairer? If I have broke anything, I'll pay for't, an it cost a pound; and so let that content for what's past, and make no more words. For what's to come, to pleasure you I'm willing to marry my cousin; so pray let's all be friends. She and I are agreed upon the matter, before a witness.

LADY WISHFORT

How's this, dear niece? Have I any comfort? Can this be true?

MILLAMANT

I am content to be a sacrifice to your repose, madam; and to convince you that I had no hand in the plot, as you were misinformed, I have laid my commands on Mirabell to come in person and be a witness that I give my hand to this flower of knighthood; and, for the contract that passed between Mirabell and me, I have obliged him to make a resignation of it in your ladyship's presence. He is without and waits your leave for admittance.

LADY WISHFORT

Well, I'll swear I am something revived at this testimony of your obedience, but I cannot admit that traitor—I fear I cannot fortify myself to support his appearance. He is as terrible to me as a Gorgon; if I see him, I fear I shall turn to stone, petrify incessantly.

MILLAMANT

If you disoblige him he may resent your refusal and insist upon the contract still; then 'tis the last time he will be offensive to you.

LADY WISHFORT

Are you sure it will be the last time? If I were sure of that—shall I never see him again?

285 *in disguise* intoxicated

307 *Gorgon* three mythical ladies with snakes instead of hair whose look had the power to petrify. Perseus slew one of them, Medusa.

MILLAMANT

Sir Wilfull, you and he are to travel together, are you not?

SIR WILFULL

'Sheart, the gentleman's a civil gentleman, aunt, let him come in. Why, we are sworn brothers and fellow travellers. We are to be Pylades and Orestes, he and I; he is to be my interpreter in foreign parts. He has been overseas once already; and with proviso, that I marry my cousin, will cross 'em once again, only to bear me company. 'Sheart, I'll call him in. An I set on't once, he shall come in—and see who'll hinder him! *Exit*

MRS. MARWOOD

This is precious fooling, if it would pass, but I'll know the bottom of it.

LADY WISHFORT

Oh dear Marwood, you are not going?

MRS. MARWOOD

Not far, madam; I'll return immediately. *Exit*

Enter SIR WILFULL *and* MIRABELL

SIR WILFULL

Look up man, I'll stand by you; 'sbud, an she do frown, she can't kill you! Besides—harkee—she dare not frown desperately, because her face is none of her own. 'Sheart, an she should, her forehead would wrinkle like the coat of a cream cheese; but mum for that, fellow traveller.

MIRABELL

If a deep sense of the many injuries I have offered to so good a lady, with a sincere remorse, and a hearty contrition, can but obtain the least glance of compassion, I am too happy. Ah madam, there was a time—but let it be forgotten—I confess I have deservedly forefeited the high place I once held, of sighing at your feet. Nay, kill me not by turning from me in disdain—I come not to plead for favour, nay, not for pardon—I am a suppliant only for your pity. I am going where I never shall behold you more—

327 *an she* Q1 (and she Q2, Ww)
339 *for your pity* Q1, Q2 (for pity Ww)

---

317 *Pylades and Orestes* famous friends and travelling companions in Greek myth and in the dramatisation of the Orestes story by Aeschylus

330–1 *coat of a cream cheese* a fine image, perhaps suggested by Jonson, *Every Man Out Of His Humour*, I, ii, 58–9: 'looke with a good startch't face, and ruffle your brow like a new boot'

SIR WILFULL

How, fellow traveller? You shall go by yourself then!

MIRABELL

Let me be pitied first, and afterwards forgotten. I ask no more.

SIR WILFULL

By'r Lady, a very reasonable request, and will cost you nothing, aunt. Come, come, forgive and forget, aunt. Why, you must an you are a Christian.

MIRABELL

Consider, madam, in reality, you could not receive much prejudice. It was an innocent device, though I confess it had a face of guiltiness. It was at most an artifice which love contrived, and errors which love produces have ever been accounted venial. At least think it is punishment enough that I have lost what in my heart I hold most dear; that to your cruel indignation I have offered up this beauty, and with her my peace and quiet, nay, all my hopes of future comfort.

SIR WILFUL

An he does not move me, would I might never be o' the Quorum! An it were not as good a deed as to drink, to give her to him again, I would I might never take shipping! Aunt, if you don't forgive quickly, I shall melt, I can tell you that. My contract went no further than a little mouth-glue, and that's hardly dry; one doleful sigh more from my fellow traveller, and 'tis dissolved.

LADY WISHFORT

Well, nephew, upon your account—ah, he has a false insinuating tongue—well sir, I will stifle my just resentment at my nephew's request, I will endeavour what I can to forget, but on proviso that you resign the contract with my niece immediately.

MIRABELL

It is in writing and with papers of concern, but I have sent my servant for it, and will deliver it to you with all acknowledgements for your transcendent goodness.

LADY WISHFORT (*Aside*)

Oh he has witchcraft in his eyes and tongue! When I did not

356 *would I might* Q1, Q2 (would I may Ww)

357 *Quorum.* To be 'of the Quorum' meant to be a Justice of the Peace.
360 *mouth-glue.* It was only an oral promise.

see him I could have bribed a villain to his assassination; but his appearance rakes the embers which have so long lain smothered in my breast.

Enter FAINALL *and* MRS. MARWOOD

FAINALL

Your date of deliberation, madam, is expired. Here is the instrument; are you prepared to sign?

LADY WISHFORT

If I were prepared, I am not empowered. My niece exerts a lawful claim, having matched herself by my direction to Sir Wilfull.

FAINALL

That sham is too gross to pass on me, though 'tis imposed on you, madam.

MILLAMANT

Sir, I have given my consent.

MIRABELL

And sir, I have resigned my pretensions.

SIR WILFULL

And sir, I assert my right, and will maintain it in defiance of you, sir, and of your instrument. 'Sheart, an you talk of an instrument, sir, I have an old fox by my thigh shall hack your instrument of ram vellum to shreds, sir! It shall not be sufficient for a *mittimus* or a tailor's measure! Therefore withdraw your instrument sir, or by'r Lady I shall draw mine.

LADY WISHFORT

Hold, nephew, hold.

MILLAMANT

Good Sir Wilfull, respite your valour.

FAINALL

Indeed, are you provided of a guard, with your single Beefeater there? But I'm prepared for you, and insist upon my first proposal. You shall submit your own estate to my

393 *a guard* Q1 (your guard Q2, Ww)

386 *fox* sword

387 *ram vellum* parchment made from sheepskin

388 *mittimus* order to the keeper of a prison to receive and keep the individual specified in the warrant

388 *tailor's measure* a parchment strip, like a modern tape measure, with measurements marked along it

394 *Beefeater* a yeoman of the guard, proverbial for bulk and strength; also used insultingly to mean 'fat menial'

management, and absolutely make over my wife's to my sole use, as pursuant to the purport and tenor of this other covenant. I suppose madam [*to* MILLAMANT] your consent is not requisite in this case, nor, Mr. Mirabell, your resignation, nor, Sir Wilfull, your right. You may draw your fox if you please, sir, and make a bear-garden flourish somewhere else—for here it will not avail. This, my Lady Wishfort, must be subscribed, or your darling daughter's turned adrift like a leaky hulk to sink or swim, as she and the current of this lewd town can agree.

LADY WISHFORT

Is there no means, no remedy, to stop my ruin? Ungrateful wretch! Dost thou not owe thy being, thy subsistence, to my daughter's fortune?

FAINALL

I'll answer you when I have the rest of it in my possession.

MIRABELL

But that you would not accept of a remedy from my hands—I own I have not deserved you should owe any obligation to me, or else, perhaps, I could advise—

LADY WISHFORT

Oh what, what? To save me and my child from ruin, from want, I'll forgive all that's past, nay, I'll consent to anything to come, to be delivered from this tyranny.

MIRABELL

Ay madam, but that is too late; my reward is intercepted; you have disposed of her who only could have made me a compensation for all my services—but be it as it may. I am resolved I'll serve you, you shall not be wronged in this savage manner.

LADY WISHFORT

How! Dear Mr. Mirabell, can you be so generous at last? But it is not possible. Harkee, I'll break my nephew's match, you shall have my niece yet and all her fortune, if you can but save me from this imminent danger.

MIRABELL

Will you? I take you at your word. I ask no more. I must have leave for two criminals to appear.

LADY WISHFORT

Ay, ay, anybody, anybody.

401 *bear-garden flourish* behaviour suited to the gross and crudely violent atmosphere in which bear-baitings took place; with a subsidiary allusion to the old-fashioned, Elizabethan impulse of Sir Wilfull to use his sword

MIRABELL
Foible is one, and a penitent.

Enter MRS. FAINALL, FOIBLE, *and* MINCING

MRS. MARWOOD (*to* FAINALL)
Oh my shame! These corrupt things are bought and brought hither to expose me. 430

MIRABELL *and* LADY WISHFORT *go to* MRS. FAINALL *and* FOIBLE

FAINALL
If it must all come out, why, let 'em know it, 'tis but the way of the world. That shall not urge me to relinquish or abate one tittle of my terms, no, I will insist the more.

FOIBLE
Yes indeed madam, I'll take my Bible oath of it.

MINCING
And so will I, mem. 435

LADY WISHFORT
Oh Marwood, Marwood, art thou false? My friend deceive me? Hast thou been a wicked accomplice with that profligate man?

MRS. MARWOOD
Have you so much ingratitude and injustice to give credit against your friend to the aspersions of two such mercenary 440 trulls?

MINCING
Mercenary mem? I scorn your words. 'Tis true we found you and Mr. Fainall in the blue garret; by the same token, you swore us to secrecy upon Messalina's poems. Mercenary? No, if we would have been mercenary we should have held 445 our tongues; you would have bribed us sufficiently.

FAINALL
Go, you are an insignificant thing. Well, what are you the better for this? Is this Mr. Mirabell's expedient? I'll be put off no longer. You thing that was a wife shall smart for this— I will not leave thee wherewithal to hide thy shame. Your 450 body shall be naked as your reputation.

429 *bought and brought* Q1, Q2 (brought Ww)

444 *Messalina.* The notoriously licentious wife of the Roman emperor Claudius could have inspired a collection of obscene poems, though there is no record of one at the time; but Mincing may be mispronouncing 'Miscellany'.

MRS. FAINALL

I despise you and defy your malice. You have aspersed me wrongfully; I have proved your falsehood. Go, you and your treacherous—I will not name it—but starve together, perish! 455

FAINALL

Not while you are worth a groat! Indeed, my dear madam, I'll be fooled no longer.

LADY WISHFORT

Ah Mr. Mirabell, this is small comfort, the detection of this affair.

MIRABELL

Oh in good time; your leave for the other offender and 460 penitent to appear, madam.

Enter WAITWELL *with a box of writings*

LADY WISHFORT

Oh, Sir Rowland! Well, rascal?

WAITWELL

What your ladyship pleases. I have brought the black box at last, madam.

MIRABELL

Give it me. Madam, you remember your promise? 465

LADY WISHFORT

Ay, dear sir.

MIRABELL

Where are the gentlemen?

WAITWELL

At hand sir, rubbing their eyes—just risen from sleep.

FAINALL

'Sdeath what's this to me? I'll not wait your private concerns.

Enter PETULANT *and* WITWOUD

PETULANT

How now, what's the matter? Whose hand's out? 470

WITWOUD

Heyday! What, are you all got together like players at the end of the last act?

MIRABELL

You may remember gentlemen, I once requested your hands as witnesses to a certain parchment.

456 *groat* coin of derisory low value

470 *Whose hand's out* reminiscent of *2 Henry IV*, II, i, 40–41, when Falstaff exclaims 'How now! Whose mare's dead? What's the matter?'

WITWOUD

Ay, I do, my hand, I remember—Petulant set his mark. 475

MIRABELL

You wrong him, his name is fairly written, as shall appear. You do not remember, gentlemen, anything of what that parchment contained?

(*undoing the box*)

WITWOUD

No.

PETULANT

Not I. I writ. I read nothing. 480

MIRABELL

Very well, now you shall know. Madam, your promise.

LADY WISHFORT

Ay, ay, sir, upon my honour.

MIRABELL

Mr. Fainall, it is now time that you should know that your lady, while she was at her own disposal, and before you had by your insinuations wheedled her out of a pretended settlement of the greatest part of her fortune— 485

FAINALL

Sir! Pretended!

MIRABELL

Yes sir. I say that this lady, while a widow, having it seems received some cautions respecting your inconstancy and tyranny of temper, which from her own partial opinion 490 and fondness of you she could never have suspected—she did, I say, by the wholesome advice of friends and of sages learned in the laws of this land, deliver this same as her act and deed to me in trust, and to the uses within mentioned. You may read if you please, (*holding out the parchment*) 495 though perhaps what is inscribed on the back may serve your occasions.

FAINALL

Very likely, sir. What's here? Damnation! (*reads*) 'A deed of conveyance of the whole estate real of Arabella Languish widow, in trust to Edward Mirabell'. Confusion! 500

MIRABELL

Even so sir, 'tis the way of the world, sir, of the widows of the world. I suppose this deed may bear an elder date than what you have obtained from your lady.

496 *inscribed* Q1, Q2 (written Ww)

499 *conveyance* the written instrument for legal transference of real property

FAINALL

Perfidious fiend! Then thus I'll be revenged!

Offers to run at MRS. FAINALL

SIR WILFULL

Hold sir, now you may make your bear-garden flourish somewhere else, sir.

FAINALL

Mirabell, you shall hear of this, sir, be sure you shall: let me pass, oaf! *Exit*

MRS. FAINALL

Madam, you seem to stifle your resentment; you had better give it vent.

MRS. MARWOOD

Yes it shall have vent, and to your confusion, or I'll perish in the attempt. *Exit*

LADY WISHFORT

Oh daughter, daughter, 'tis plain thou hast inherited thy mother's prudence.

MRS. FAINALL

Thank Mr. Mirabell, a cautious friend, to whose advice all is owing.

LADY WISHFORT

Well Mr. Mirabell, you have kept your promise, and I must perform mine. First I pardon for your sake Sir Rowland there, and Foible; the next thing is to break the matter to my nephew—and how to do that—

MIRABELL

For that, madam, give yourself no trouble, let me have your consent. Sir Wilfull is my friend, he has had compassion upon lovers and generously engaged a volunteer in this action, for our service, and now designs to prosecute his travels.

SIR WILFULL

'Sheart aunt I have no mind to marry. My cousin's a fine lady, and the gentleman loves her and she loves him, and they deserve one another. My resolution is to see foreign parts—I have set on't—and when I'm set on't, I must do't—and if these two gentlemen would travel too, I think they may be spared.

PETULANT

For my part, I say little; I think things are best off or on.

WITWOUD

Egad I understand nothing of the matter; I'm in a maze yet, like a dog in a dancing school.

LADY WISHFORT

Well sir, take her, and with her all the joy I can give you. 535

MILLAMANT

Why does not the man take me? Would you have me give myself to you over again?

MIRABELL

Ay, and over and over again, for (*kisses her hand*) I would have you as often as possibly I can. Well, heaven grant I love you not too well, that's all my fear. 540

SIR WILFULL

'Sheart you'll have time enough to toy after you're married; or, if you will toy now, let us have a dance in the mean time, that we, who are not lovers, may have some other employment besides looking on.

MIRABELL

With all my heart, dear Sir Wilfull; what shall we do for 545 music?

FOIBLE

Oh sir, some that were provided for Sir Rowland's entertainment are yet within call.

A dance

LADY WISHFORT

As I am a person I can hold out no longer. I have wasted my spirits so today already, that I am ready to sink under the 550 fatigue; and I cannot but have some fears upon me yet that my son Fainall will pursue some desperate course.

MIRABELL

Madam, disquiet not yourself on that account; to my knowledge his circumstances are such, he must of force comply. For my part I will contribute all that in me lies 555 to a reunion. In the mean time, madam (*to* MRS. FAINALL) let me, before these witnesses, restore to you this deed of trust. It may be a means, well managed, to make you live easily together.

From hence let those be warned, who mean to wed, 560
Lest mutual falsehood stain the bridal bed;
For each deceiver to his cost may find
That marriage frauds, too oft, are paid in kind. *Exeunt*

538 *for* (omitted Q2, Ww)
541 *have time enough* ed. (have him time enough Q1, Q2)

---

541 *toy* embrace

EPILOGUE

Spoken by Mrs. Bracegirdle

After our Epilogue this crowd dismisses,
I'm thinking how this play'll be pulled to pieces.
But pray consider, ere you doom its fall,
How hard a thing 'twould be to please you all.
There are some critics so with spleen diseased 5
They scarcely come inclining to be pleased;
And sure he must have more than mortal skill
Who pleases anyone against his will.
Then, all bad poets, we are sure, are foes,
And how their number's swelled, the town well knows. 10
In shoals I've marked 'em judging in the pit,
Though they're on no pretence for judgement fit,
But that they have been damned, for want of wit.
Since when they, by their own offences taught,
Set up for spies on plays, and finding fault. 15
Others there are whose malice we'd prevent;
Such who watch plays with scurrilous intent
To mark out who by characters are meant,
And though no perfect likeness they can trace
Yet each pretends to know the copied face. 20
These with false glosses feed their own ill nature,
And turn to libel, what was meant a satire.
May such malicious fops this fortune find,
To think themselves alone the fools designed,
If any are so arrogantly vain 25
To think they singly can support a scene
And furnish fool enough to entertain.
For well the learned and the judicious know
That satire scorns to stoop so meanly low,
As any one abstracted fop to show. 30
For as when painters form a matchless face
They, from each fair one, catch some different grace,

2 *I'm* ed. (In Q1)

---

21 *glosses* explanatory notes
30 *abstracted* specially chosen from his fellows

And shining features in one portrait blend,
To which no single beauty must pretend;
So poets oft do in one piece expose 35
Whole *belles assemblées* of coquettes and beaux.

FINIS